DOROTHY AND LILLIAN GISH

DOROTHY AND LILLIAN GISH

❧ By Lillian Gish ❧

EDITED BY

James E. Frasher

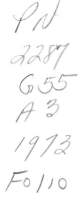
CHARLES SCRIBNER'S SONS/NEW YORK

THIS BOOK PUBLISHED SIMULTANEOUSLY IN
THE UNITED STATES OF AMERICA AND IN CANADA—
COPYRIGHT UNDER THE BERNE CONVENTION

1 3 5 7 9 11 13 15 17 19 RD/C 20 18 16 14 12 10 8 6 4 2

PRINTED IN THE UNITED STATES OF AMERICA
Library of Congress Catalog Card Number: 73-1111
SBN 684-13571-X

To Mary Robinson McConnell Gish

OUR WISE AND BELOVED MOTHER

Acknowledgments

The majority of the photographs contained in this book are from the Private Collections of Dorothy and Lillian Gish, which are bequeathed to the Library of Congress, Washington, D.C.

I am so thankful for the generous help of British Dominion, Columbia Pictures, Walt Disney Productions, Lynx Film-United Motion Picture Organization, Metro-Goldwyn-Mayer, Inc., Paramount Pictures, David O. Selznick Productions, Twentieth Century-Fox Film Corporation, United Artists Corporation, Universal Pictures,

Daniel Taradash, President, and the Academy of Motion Picture Arts and Sciences, The John Patrick Collection—Boston University, The British Film Institute, The George Eastman House—Rochester, The Walter Hampden Memorial Library at The Players, The Library of Congress, Eileen Bowser, Associate Curator, Department of Film—The Museum of Modern Art, Melvin Parks, Curator, and Mary Merrill, Theatre and Music Collection—The Museum of the City of New York, Paul Myers, Curator, Theatre Collection—The New York Public Library, Astor, Lenox and Tilden Foundation, Playbill Magazine, a Division of Metromedia, Inc.,

and
Brooks Atkinson,
Mrs. Schiller Aikens, Hugh Beaumont, DeWitt Bodeen, Gilbert Cates, George Cukor, Nell Dorr, William K. Everson, Lottie Frasher, Ben Hartigan, Dr. Otto Kallir, Lucy Kroll, Emmet Lavery, Armina Marshall, Laura McCullaugh, Burroughs Mitchell, Gene Ringgold, Herb Sterne, H. Steven Vasquez, Herbert Wilcox, Mrs. Virginia Wortman,
and
our gifted art editor,
Margareta F. Lyons,
who must have a third eye.

Contents

Author's Note

In the early era of films cast members were not identified on still photographs and due to the tricks one's memory can play, I humbly apologize to my fellow players who are unidentified.

DOROTHY AND LILLIAN GISH

THE BEGINNING

*T*HERE were hundreds of theatres across the country in the beginning of this century. Successful plays opened in New York, ran five or six months, then finished the season playing other cities. Vaudeville and burlesque were replacing minstrels. Jazz was introduced by Negro bands in Southern towns. The Ziegfeld Follies began. People flocked to free bandstands or paid to hear John Philip Sousa. Melodramas charging 10-20-30¢ a seat flourished everywhere. Actors were certain of forty weeks work in them if they were willing to play onenight stands. New competition was threatening: empty stores were rented, filled with benches or chairs, a piano, a white sheet, and a projection machine. You paid 5¢ for a thirty-minute show in places called nickelodeons.

4

Grandmother Diana Waltz Gish

Grandfather David Gish

Our Great Grandparents
Grandfather and Grandmother Waltz

THE GISH GENEALOGY

*Mama's family considered Papa's people upstarts because her first
ancestor, Francis Bernard, left England in 1632 for America. He
settled in Hadley, Massachusetts.*

*The first Gish left Germany (the Mosel Valley) in 1733. He,
Matthais Gish, arrived in Philadelphia on board "The Philadephia
Merchant" in September and was given a landgrant in Penryn,
Lancaster County.*

*A hundred and fifty years later six families left those parts to-
gether by train from Harrisburg bound for Abilene, Kansas. Among*

Papa James Leigh Gish

Four Generations
Diana Waltz Gish   Our Grandmother
Mary McConnell Gish   Our Mother
Lillian Diana Gish   Me
Emily Ward Robinson   Our Great Grandmother

Emily Ward Robinson McConnell.
When Mama was a baby her
Mother died at the age of twenty-
eight leaving four children.

President Zachary Taylor, a relative
on Mother's side. This painting
hangs in my dining room.

Grandmother Emily Ward Robinson McConnell and Grandfather
Henry Clay McConnell

Mama Mary Robinson McConnell

them were the Reverend Benjamin Gish and the Reverend Jacob Eisenhower, Dwight David's grandfather.

The Gishes settled on one side of Turkey Creek which runs into Smokey Hill and the Eisenhowers on the other.

Mama's most distinguished forebearer was Zachary Taylor, known as "Old Rough and Ready," the twelfth President of the United States.

On Papa's side, Oliver Holmes Gish won distinction as a geophysicist with the Carnegie Institute in Washington, D.C.

Dorothy and I were most fortunate in our choice of ancestors and "upstart" became an important part of our careers.

Uncle Harry McConnell

Aunt Emily Ward McConnell

Uncle Frank McConnell

Papa's confectionery shop in Baltimore

Gish & Meixner—a summer stand in an amusement park

Holding my cup at Grandmother's pump

Dorothy Elizabeth Gish

When Papa spent the money that Mother had saved to pay for the furniture, our lives changed.

Mama (May Bernard) as a member of Proctor's Stock Company giving her self-conscious impression of an actress

Papa with whiskers trying to look older

Dolores Greene and Dorothy

When Mother decided to go on alone with her two children she found a job playing small parts and soon two actresses became our lodgers. One of them, Alice Niles, told her she could get work with a western traveling company of "In Convict's Stripes" if she had a little girl. I made my debut in Rising Sun, Ohio, and took my first curtain call on the shoulders of the handsome leading man, Walter Huston.

Later that year our other lodger, Dolores Greene, secured a part in a southern company of "East Lynne" and Dorothy became "Little Willie."

Mother made all of our clothes by hand—a talent neither Dorothy nor I inherited.

Between matinee and evening we were allowed to play "house" on the unused stage. Dorothy as the "lady of the manor."

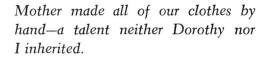

"Doatsie"

Dorothy's chocolate   and vanilla expressions

Our treat was a shared ice cream soda.

The touring melodramas used painted posters so no company pictures were taken. Our ten dollar a week salary prohibited all non-essentials. Our only stills came from photographers who paid us five dollars a day to pose for them—which meant food and rent for a week.

Posing with a model for the cover of Burr McIntosh's picture magazine

The only acting lesson we ever had: "Speak loud and clear or they'll get another little girl."

Teddy

HER FIRST FALSE STEP

The first year we appeared in this melodrama there were parts for both of us. The villain threw me into the lion's cage with Teddy and Jenny. The following season, to save expenses, they cut the part of one child and I went on to another play while Dorothy replaced me. Once we all played the same town but had different matinees so I could go backstage with Mother. Although I had had no fear of Teddy and Jenny, when they threw Dorothy into the lion's cage Mother said I ran crying to the dressing room, covering my ears with clothing so I could not hear the roars. The following year Teddy and Jenny went back to work in the circus and Jenny tore an arm off her trainer.

Helen Ray, our beautiful leading woman, holding Dorothy in her arms and me by the hand

Our first gift from admirers was perfume which Mother refused to let us use on our skin or clothes. Being practical we put it in our shoes. The soles fell off.

LITTLE GIRL FLUNG INTO LIONS' CAGE

Small Actress Tells The Junior Editor How It Feels.

SHE'S NOT A BIT AFRAID

And how would you, Master Junior, or Miss Junior, like to be flung into a cage of lions? To be close enough to their great, hungry-looking mouths to feel big waves of breath almost strong enough to take you off your feet, to be close enough to their blazing eyes to think that those eyes were

DOROTHY GISH.

really balls of fire? It would be a frightful thing, wouldn't it? But there is a little girl—Dorothy Gish—a wee play actress at the Grand, who has this very thing happen to her every night in the week.

You see, in the play in which this all takes place, Dorothy's papa is supposed to be a very bad, unkind sort of a man, and he throws his baby girl into a den of lions so that she may be killed. Then a brave man, the hero of the play, jumps into the cage and saves her. There is no make-believe about this part of the play. The lions, two of them, are really there, fierce, big creatures they are, too, and little Dorothy is really tossed right at their feet.

To be sure she is only there while you could count 20, but a lot of unpleasant things might happen in a lions' cage before you could get even that far along with your counting.

Feeling sure that the Juniors would like to know just how a little girl would feel if she found herself almost in the mouths of hungry looking lions, The Junior editor went to the Grand Wednesday afternoon to see what Miss Dorothy herself had to say about it.

After the manager of the company had introduced "Miss Dorothy Gish" just as if she were a grown-up, instead of a baby girl of 5, and after Miss Dorothy had shaken hands, just like a grown-up might have done, then she was asked to please tell The Daily News Juniors just how much afraid a little girl is when so very near a big lion. And right there The Junior editor had a big surprise. For that wee little girl, who wouldn't make a good toothful for an ordinary lion, solemnly declared, and she solemnly shook her yellow curls, so that you'd know she was telling the truth—that she "isn't one single bit 'fraid of the lions."

"Because," explained Dorothy for the benefit of doubting Juniors, "they know me. They are very cross, specially Teddy—Jennie is not quite so bad—but I just give them lumps of sugar, say nice things to them, never tease them, so they know I like them, and they like me. It doesn't hurt a bit to be flung into the cage, and I'm not afraid."

Then Miss Dorothy told The Daily News Junior that she was almost 6, that she had been on the stage three years, that she just loves the stage, and that she is going to be an actress all her life.

Through the Side Door
By FRITZY.

Wonder if Brown of uncertain identity which we are to see next week is Buster's papa? Too bad the small son leaves just as his parent is arriving.

Edith Evelyn is appearing as an elegant and genteel cook over at the Academy.

LITTLE DOROTHY.

Did you ever see De Wolf Hopper and Marguerite Clark taking a promenade down the street together? It's a whole show in itself.

Supt. R. D. Whitehead of the Humane society isn't quite sure but that he will have something to say about little Dorothy and her lion act at the Bijou. The child, who cannot be more than 7 or 8 years old, is allowed to enter a cage in which are two ramping, roaring kings of the forest. To be sure, she doesn't go in very far and the lions remain at the other end of the cage, but still there is always the chance that they may turn and rend her. Supt. Whitehead is going to investigate and if he decides that it is inhumanity to children to allow Little Dorothy to run the risk, the wicked papa in the play will be obliged to forego at least one of his evil tricks.

For this bad man, you see, wants to make terms with his wife to which she will not accede, and he hits upon the scheme of thrusting her beloved daughter into the lion's den to bring her to agreement.

To a mere acquaintance the lions look pacific enough but such an intimate friend of theirs as the press agent assures us that familiarity with a lion breeds but short-lived contempt. During the recent engagement in Chicago, he relates, a woman member of the company, though repeatedly warned to keep away, put her hand through the bars and stroked one of the big beasts. He paid not the slightest attention, and, emboldened by her success, the next night she invited another member of the company to watch her do the lion-taming act.

"See, it's quite safe," she cried, but even as she spoke, the lion's paw shot suddenly through the bars and caught her in the side. Fortunately her dress gave way but not before the sharp claws had drawn blood.

Well, well!

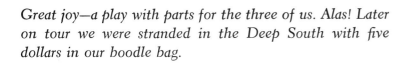

Great joy—a play with parts for the three of us. Alas! Later on tour we were stranded in the Deep South with five dollars in our boodle bag.

NEW STAR THEATRE
LEXINGTON AVENUE AND 107th STREET.
WM. T. KEOGH AMUSEMENT COMPANY, - - - OWNERS.

Week Commencing Monday Matinee, October 26
Matinees Monday, Wednesday and Saturday.

HARRY MARTELL Presents
EDWARD ESMONDE
In the Romantic Comedy-Drama,
AT DUTY'S CALL.
By SI. U. COLLINS.

Characters in the Prologue, 1863.
Henry Hooker, Jr., age 40.....................Edward Esmonde
Martha Hooker, his wife.........................Louise Lander
Clara Hooker, his daughter......................Lillian Gish
Henry Hooker, his cousin........................A. G. Carleton
Mrs. Henry Hooker...............................Jane Moran
Williams Judkins, age 25........................William Lloyd
Charles Simms, U. S. A..........................Laurence Finch
Mrs. Jane Snaggs................................Genevieve McCloud
Simon Snaggs, her son, age 15...................Walter B. Gilbert
Amanda Jenks....................................May Benard
Abner Harris....................................Harry Fowler

Characters in the Play, 1898.
Old Jim, the soldier of Propville................Edward Esmonde
Clara King, a widow (Clara Hooker of the Prologue)...Mona Carrington
Alice King, her daughter........................Louise Lander
Mary King, her daughter.........................Baby Florence
Paul Camden, a young minister...................Laurence Finch
John Hooker, son of Henry Hooker of the Prologue....A. G. Carleton
William Judkins, age 60.........................William Lloyd
Simon Snaggs, age 50............................Walter B. Gilbert
Suzette, a maid.................................Genevieve McCloud
Ephraim Jackson, Hooker's discharged servant...Harry Fowler
James Locke, the town constable................William J. King
Silas Blake, postmaster of Propville...........Ben F. T.

Every year we hoped we would play Richmond, Virginia. Not only was there a park, Capitol Square, full of squirrels where five cents worth of peanuts lasted long enough to make friends, but also there was a boarding house that served chicken, ham, and fish at one meal. Luxury!

With our producer's wife, Mrs. Ed Schiller, and an unidentified man on the beach in front of the boardwalk in Atlantic City. Mr. Schiller later held an important position with MGM.

Dorothy on tour in St. Paul, Minnesota

My Dear Mr Ferris

I have started several times to write to you but could never write a letter to suit. But mamma says I have to send this one. But you must excuse my mistakes and bad writing. Our season closed 2 weeks ago and I am visiting my my aunt. Am Dorothy and I are having a fine time playing in the yard I do wish we could get in a company with you next season. should I send our pictures to you in D ender or will you send me your route. will have no more news so I will close write same. with love and kisses

your loving frind

2 Lillian 9

the little pocket book and card you sent me were beatiful and I thank you sa much for them I will keep them to remember you by

An early thank-you note. Neither my penmanship, my spelling, nor my promptness has improved much.

MELL FARIS

BUSINESS MANAGER
"HER FIRST FALSE STEP."

When there was time we always explored the towns on tour. New England, Pennsylvania, and the South were rich in history. Our reward for learning our lessons would be visiting the local cemetery searching for the names of our ancestors—our favorite game.

FISKE O'HARA IN "DION O'DARE"

Irish Tenor in "Rose Song" and His "Aids" as Seen by Cartoonist Harris.

MRS O'DARE, DION'S MOTHER

HARRIS

FISKE O'HARA AS DION O'DARE

LITTLE GILLIE

SCENE ACT I

Academy — Fiske O'Hara in "Dion O'Dare."

Fiske O'Hara and his company received a royal welcome last night at the Academy. "Dion O'Dare" is an Irish melodrama rather out of the ordinary, its villains being less detestable than usual, while the romance of Dion O'Dare, the poor sculptor who falls in love with the rich young woman is naturally worked out, and, of course, happily ended. Mr. Fiske, who played the title role, captured his audience from the start, and his songs, particularly the old ones, "Wearing of the Green" and "Believe Me, if All These Endearing Young Charms," were loudly applauded. In response to repeated calls, Mr. O'Hara made an address of thanks.

The company is excellent, all the parts being well played. Florence Malone and Marie Quinn, who play the leading feminine roles, left little to be desired, and with little Dorothy Gish, who took the part of a child, shared with Mr. O'Hara in the generous applause.

Fiske O'Hara delighted enthusiastic audiences at the National Theater yesterday with "Dion O'Dare," a charming drama of Irish life of a bygone generation. The plot is just sufficient to keep the story of the play connected, but it is interest compelling from its very simplicity. Mr. O'Hara's singing took his hearers by storm. He has an excelent company, among whom should be mentioned Dorothy Gish, the best child character actress Rochester has seen in many a day; Florence Malone as Mary Kyle, the heiress, and Thornton Cole, in the role of Algernon Goldingay.

The cast is uniformally excellent. Little Dorothy Gish is quite the cleverest child actress that has appeared in Minneapolis for a long time. She possesses a naturalness and lack of conscious restraint that makes her work stand out.

Miss Dorothy Gish, who plays the part of Gillie Morgan, is one of the daintiest and sweetest little actresses seen here in a long time, and her work is admirable. Especial mention is due Miss Florence Malone and Miss Marie Quinn.

ROBERT T. HAINES (JAMES CLARK) & LILLIAN NEWTON (DOROTHY GISH)

THE HERO DECLARES HIS LOVE

Dorothy Gish

Fisk O'Hara Co.

Dorothy's first great love was Fiske O'Hara. When he married his leading lady, Marie Quinn, Dorothy's seven-year-old heart burst and she couldn't eat for three weeks.

"The Good Little Devil" was a David Belasco production. I'm at
the left with Wilda Bennett, Claire Burke, Mary Pickford, Regina
Wallace, Georgia Fursman, and Edna Griffin. Clare Booth
Luce was Mary's understudy.

Our upstairs neighbors, the Charlie Murrays, were
famous vaudevillians. She kindly loaned me her
fur for posing.

These were the melodramas in which we appeared:
"In Convict's Stripes"
two versions of "East Lynne"
"Her First False Step"
"At Duty's Call"
"Dion O'Dare"
"The Coward"
"Editha's Burglar"
"Little Red Schoolhouse"
"Volunteer Organist"
"The Truth Tellers"
"Mr. Blarney from Ireland"
"The Child Wife"
and with Sarah Bernhardt's Company

It would be seventeen years before I stepped on the legitimate stage again.

FIRST DECADE

*V*AUDEVILLE reached its peak, then declined. The legitimate theatre continued to flourish with many famous stars. Supper clubs were becoming popular and Tin Pan Alley introduced ragtime. Irene Castle caused women everywhere to bob their hair, brought in a new style of dancing, and slenderness became the vogue. "The Birth of a Nation" was the first feature-length film to be made, attracting three times the population of the towns where it played. Little melodramas and nickelodeons disappeared, to be replaced by film cathedrals holding thousands. Actor's Equity was formed. World War I erupted, followed in 1917 by the outbreak of Spanish influenza which killed more people than the war. At the end of these two tragedies we were left with Prohibition and a new way of life.

AN UNSEEN ENEMY   1912

During the summers we shared an apartment with the Smith family to save money while our Mothers looked for work in the coming theatrical season. One day when we were on tour Dorothy and I rushed to our boarding house to tell Mother we had just seen Gladys Smith in a moving picture. She wondered what terrible misfortune had befallen the Smiths that Gladys had to go into the movies to make a living. On our return to New York we went to the Biograph Studio to inquire about their hardship.

When someone they called "Little Mary" came into the small office she told us that they had changed their name to Pickford, that all four, Mother, sister Lottie, brother Jack, and herself, were all working in films making the enormous amount of two hundred seventy-five a week. When she introduced us to—we thought Mr. Biograph—he asked us if we would like to be part of an audience scene he was about to make. Mother, Dorothy, and I would get five dollars—each. Later that afternoon he asked us to rehearse a story that needed two sisters. Upstairs we found Henry Walthall, Bobby Harron, and Lionel Barrymore waiting.

Meanwhile we learned that D. W. Griffith was the director's real name. He said he wanted to see if we could act. Since words meant nothing, he soon took a gun out of his pocket and began chasing us around the room firing at the ceiling. We were sure we were in an insane asylum.

Then he changed our hair ribbons to red and blue so he could tell us apart. Dorothy he called red, I was blue, when we filmed "An Unseen Enemy" a few days later, but not without Mother at our side. She tried to ease our fears by telling us that with a Barrymore in the cast they couldn't all be crazy.

ROSE

MARY

THE PERFIDY OF MARY
ROMANCE MEETS REALITY

WHAT GOT HIM "IN BAD" WITH ROSE

ROSE FINDS SOLACE IN YOUNG LOTHARIO

FATHER SHATTERS MARY'S ROMANCE

BUT MARY FINDS A WAY TO HELP HERSELF AND ROSE

IN LOVING-LAND
"WHERE ALL THE LOVES OF BYGONE AGES RENEW ETERNAL VOWS"

BIOGRAPH

BIOGRAPH

THE LADY AND THE MOUSE

AN OLD-FASHIONED ROMANCE

THE LITTLE LADY'S HEART STRUGGLE OVER THE FATE OF THE PANTRY'S UNWELCOME VISITOR AFFECTED EVERYBODY; THE TRAMP THE MOST, FOR HE MARRIED THE LITTLE LADY. IT GAVE THE LITTLE SISTER HER HEALTH, THE AUNT, AN APPRECIATION OF KINDLY ACTS AND PULLED EVERYONE'S HEARTSTRINGS.

THE CAST INCLUDES

DOROTHY GISH   LIONEL BARRYMORE   LILLIAN GISH

RELEASED APRIL 26 '13

Stories often came from a casual remark. Dorothy had been with Biograph while I was working with David Belasco in the theatre. One day the company was discussing the newcomer, me, when Mr. Griffith overheard Lionel Barrymore say that I looked as if I couldn't kill a cockroach. D. W. wrote a story around such a character, changing the roach to a mouse, and called it "The Lady and the Mouse."

BIOGRAPH

HER MOTHER'S OATH

THE STORY OF AN ORTHODOX MOTHER'S UNSPARING STAND FOR PRINCIPLE.

THE ORTHODOX MOTHER'S INDOMITABLE WILL DWARFED THE CHILD'S INDIVIDUALITY, DEFEATING THE VERY PURPOSE IT WOULD ATTAIN. THE GIRL RAN AWAY WITH AN ACTOR AND THE FEARFUL PRAYER, "IF I EVER SPEAK TO THAT MAN AGAIN, MAY GOD STRIKE MY MOTHER BLIND," WAS FULFILLED, BUT IN THE END THE WOMAN WAS SAVED FROM HERSELF.

THE CAST INCLUDES

HENRY WALTHALL

DOROTHY GISH

CHARLES HILL MAILES

RELEASED JUNE 28, 1913

Biograph was a brownstone house at 11 East 14th Street. The downstairs parlor was the studio with overhead Cooper Hewitt lights that made the faces under them look decayed or dead. Once a six weeks old baby was sent back to the orphanage with a message to please send a young looking baby. Even a photogenic face looked too old at eighteen to play heroines. Our teens were spent trying to play "old" until lighting and photography improved.

Donald Crisp, Henry Walthall, and Walter Long wearing the big moustache

THE MOUNTAIN RAT   1914

Dorothy played "Nell, the Mountain Rat" in this Reliance Special feature in four parts, filmed in California.

Dorothy was never fond of horses as she fell from a pony when she was a small child and had a compound fracture of the elbow.

Henry Walthall

Donald Crisp

First Week	Starting Monday	Fourth May

AUDITORIUM Clune's Theatre Beautiful
5th and Olive Streets
Program

D. W. GRIFFITH'S GREAT PRODUCTION OF
"HOME, SWEET HOME"

Picturing the life of John Howard Payne, author of that world famous song. Acted by the entire personnel of the Reliance and Majestic Companies.

CAST OF CHARACTERS

John Howard Payne	Henry B. Walthall
His Mother	Mrs. Crowel
His Sweetheart	Lillian Gish
His Sister	Dorothy Gish
Apple Pie Mary	Mae Marsh
Her Father	Spottiswoode Aitken
The Easterner	Robert Harron
His Fiancee	Miriam Cooper
The Brothers {	Donald Crisp / James Kirkwood
The Half-Wit	Jack Pickford
The Husband	Courtenay Foote
The Romeo	Owen Moore
The Musician	Edward Dillon
The Wife	Blanche Sweet
The Accordion Player	Geo. Berringer
The Maid	Teddy Sampson

Note—This story is told in five sectional reels, detailed in three parts.

Hearst Selig News Pictorial
CURRENT EVENTS

"The Old Fire Horse and the New Fire Chief."
A COMEDY IN TWO SECTIONS

AUDITORIUM, CLUNE'S THEATRE BEAUTIFUL
Musical Program by Augmented Orchestra
Conducted by
CARLI D. ELINOR
Famous Roumanian Violinist

CONCERT PROGRAM

Suite Americana................T. W. Thurbom
The Opera Mirror—Fantasia on favorite opera themes.
"Barber of Seville" and "Rigoletto"—a part of the Fantasia will be interpreted by the talented Mr. Edgar Stahl, in his beautiful solos.
Call Me Thine Own................L. Eclair
By Miss L. Fuhrer
Lo! Hear the Gentle Lark................Duet
Miss Victoria Percival, Flute
Mr. L. G. Guerrero, Clarinet
Hadella Overture................F. Van Flotow
Will be featured in "Home Sweet Home"

PROF. C. C. DE ROS ALSATIAN PIPE ORGANIST, WILL RENDER IMPROVISED MUSIC APPROPRIATE TO THE DIFFERENT SUBJECTS SHOWN ON THE SCREEN.

Note—Retain this program for a collection to be filed in a handsome leather case Mr. W. H. Clune will present each of his regular patrons next Christmas.

FOR SYNOPSIS SEE OTHER SIDE

Hours of Performances, 12 Noon to 11 P. M.

SYNOPSIS—"Home, Sweet Home."

PART I

John Howard Payne at home is a brilliant, lovable boy, but a trifle wild and grieving his mother and his sweetheart by his actions. He leaves to go upon the stage, the genius within him fighting for exercise.

We see him successful though dissipated. Later as a failure he flees to England where he is an actor and later as a great playwright.

Now we find him in France "'mid pleasures and palaces," and he writes the song that has reached all hearts, the immortal "Home, Sweet Home."

Disappointed in love, he died in Africa, without home, without kindred to ease his misery. His mother died believing him unworthy.

PART II—EPISODE ONE

Its music rings its way into all hearts.

A lunch counter girl in a western mining camp meets a young Easterner. They love. The call of the East reaches him, but as he leaves a peripatetic musician with an accordion calls him to his "Home, Sweet Home," in the calico-covered arms of Apple Pie Mary.

EPISODE TWO

To the business man's wife in her beautiful home comes a youthful Lothario. But a great musician playing on the floor below calls her back to her trusting mate.

EPISODE THREE

Life's stage is again shifted. Brothers quarrel and both are killed. The mother, distracted, is reconciled to a lonely life of love by the strains of "Home, Sweet Home."

EPISODE FOUR

Thus it is shown that Payne left something behind him that helped the lives of many people to be happier and brighter, and his dead mother, long before, departed to the Isles of the Blest, looks down and sees the good her son's immortal strains and words have done.

Struggling up from the depths of hell to the fairer heights of Heaven, Payne is seen, and finally finds rest above with his mother and sweetheart.

FINIS

But below on earth good is being done. The song of songs, "Home, Sweet Home," still goes on being wafted into the hearts of men and women, telling its story and bringing men and women back to their homes and their better selves.

COMING!
Next Week, Monday, May 11th,
"A MILLION BID"
From Geo. Cameron's Play "Agnes." Produced in 5 Parts by Vitagraph. This was run 250 continuous performances in New York

---

HOME SWEET HOME   1914

This film included the entire Griffith stock company and is often referred to as the first all-star picture.

When we made "Home Sweet Home" our cameras had not yet learned to move. The film ends with the hero being rescued from Hell by his young love who is now an angel and they fly off together.

Henry Walthall and I were hung up on wires in the hot sun. After we had flown past the camera, Griffith said we would have to do it another way because the last thing the audience saw was Wally's feet, looking enormous in close-up. Finally, D. W. flew us backward, away from the camera. This was taken very seriously in 1914; later of course the audience laughed. Hanging in the hot sun Wally fainted, but I enjoyed myself as I had learned about flying the year before in "The Good Little Devil."

GRANNY   1914

This story was suggested by a story from the morning newspaper.

A. T. Sears and Ida Wilkinson in the background

A. T. Sears, Ida Wilkinson, and an unidentified woman

Seated beside Dorothy,
W. E. Lawrence

DOWN THE ROAD TO CREDITVILLE 1914

Donald Crisp directed this picture. Donald, a fine actor, became a director as well. A good Scotsman, he accumulated a fortune doing both.

The handsome leading man is Wallace Reid.

BACK TO THE KITCHEN   1914

The man in the cap is Jack O'Brien. Dorothy and I worked often under his direction.

SANDS OF FATE   1914

Dorothy had two leading men, Bobby Harron and Raoul Walsh. Raoul later played Booth, the actor who shot Abraham Lincoln, in "The Birth of a Nation" and went on to direct many fine films.

Raoul Walsh   Robert Harron

Raoul Walsh standing holding his hat, Bobby Harron on one side of Dorothy, and Donald Crisp on the other

THE SAVING GRACE   1914

William Christy Cabanne graduated from a Griffith assistant to a director. I played in his first film, a western, and many others. Our family and his became close friends.

Fred Burns, here with Dorothy, and his brother, Bobby, were famous Buffalo Bill circus riders. Once in a film I made with Bobby he told me the most dangerous stunt he had ever done was when I jumped from a runaway wagon to him on horseback while both were traveling at the same speed.

George Seigmann and Fred Burns

Fred Burns

SPOTTISWOOD AITKEN

LILLIAN GISH

HENRY WALTHALL

GRIFFITH FEATURE FILM PLAYERS

BLANCHE SWEET

D.W. GRIFFITH

MUTUAL

DOROTHY GISH

MARY ALDEN

MAE MARSH

MIRIAM COOPER

GEORGE SIEGMAN

JOSEPHINE

BONAPARTE CROWELL

ROBERT HARRON

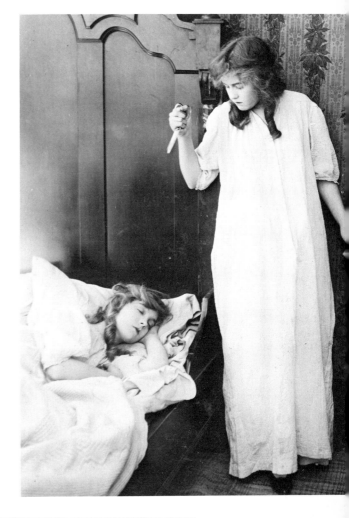

OPPOSITE. In this period if your eye was not larger than your mouth, you were not considered photogenic. Dorothy qualified with a tiny mouth. I was afraid to laugh for fear that my oversized mouth would show.

Eugene Pallette

HOW HAZEL GOT EVEN
1915

This became known as a "jinx" production. Donald Crisp started as director, became ill, and George Seigmann took over. Then Dorothy was struck by an automobile. It was Thanksgiving day and we were working. While returning to the studio from the little "white kitchen" where we lunched, Dorothy was crossing the street with Mae Marsh when a car suddenly appeared. She pushed Mae so that she wouldn't be hurt and was run down herself, resulting in the loss of one toe.

We did not know many people outside of our company but the entire industry heard of the accident and did everything they could during Dorothy's four-week convalescence. Mack Sennett sent his new comedies with a machine to run them on for her amusement. Candy, ice cream, and flowers came in daily abundance until she could return to work.

W. E. Lawrence   Fred Burns

Teddy Sampson

THE LOST LORD LOWELL
1915

Dorothy played an ill-treated maid-of-all-works who falls in love with the next-door butler. Naturally he is a rich nobleman in disguise.

Frank Bennett

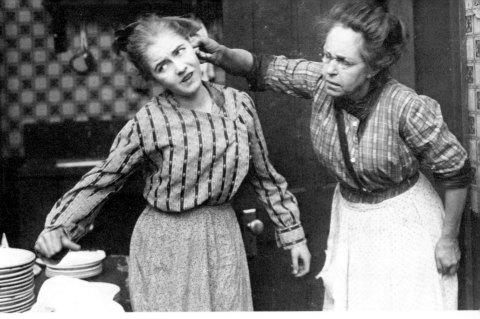

Catherine Henry

THE BIRTH OF A NATION 1915

"The Birth of a Nation" cost sixty-one thousand dollars to film. It took nine weeks to complete. Each scene was photographed only once as there was not enough money for two takes. The one exception was Mae Marsh's death scene because she had forgotten to wear the Confederate flag tied around her waist. "Huck" Wortman built the sets in violated perspective to make them seem larger and to save lumber. No more than three hundred men were used on the battlefield. Griffith filled the empty spaces with trees, smoke, and horses which helped, with only three hundred men, to give the effect of a thousand soldiers and create a whole war. Even the leading actors played other parts, some wearing burnt cork since there were no black actors in Hollywood then. Much of the time we had no money to pay the company as the extras had to be paid daily. And there was no written

Joseph Henabery as Abraham Lincoln and Ralph Lewis as the Honorable Austin Stoneman, Leader of the House. Stoneman's character was based on Thaddeus Stevens, the real villain of the story. He told the black people that he would "crush the white South under the heel of the black South."

script on "The Birth." Mr. Griffith had every scene in his head, down to the last detail.

In the morning we carried all our costumes and props that we might need as there was no time to return to our dressing rooms from the sets built all over our working lot. Freeman, an extra on the film, would help me with my hoop skirts and heavy clothes. As he stood, leaning on his gun, watching my scene at the hospital with the "Little Colonel," Griffith told Billy Bitzer to take a few feet of film of him. It proved to be the greatest laugh in the picture.

Years later, I, of all people, found myself riding on a float at the New York World's Fair. Hearing my name called, I looked down and there stood Freeman holding a dear four-year-old boy, his son, on his shoulders. The float moved away and I lost him.

Henry Walthall and Freeman

Joseph Henabery as Abraham Lincoln and Josephine Crowell as Mrs. Cameron

The battle scenes were filmed at what later became the Universal lot.

The assassination scene at Ford's Theatre, Washington, D.C.

Raoul Walsh as John Wilkes Booth leaping from the President's box. Booth caught his spur in the draped flag and broke his leg which led to his capture.

Henry Walthall as Colonel Ben Cameron with Miriam Cooper as Margaret Cameron and Elmer Clifton as her brother, Phil Stoneman, on location in Calexico, California

We played out of doors as we had no lighted studio at that time. Every scene in "The Birth" was made in natural daylight. Below one can see the canvas which we regulated to filter the light into the room.

Mary Alden as Lydia Brown, Stoneman's mulatto housekeeper

George Siegmann as Silas Lynch and Ralph Lewis as Austin Stoneman, my father

A photograph that Henry Walthall carried before he ever met me. He was supposed to fall in love with her picture. I posed "live" within the frame because that was the fastest way to do it.

45

As Elsie Stoneman

Mae Marsh as the adorable Little Sister

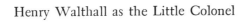

Henry Walthall as the Little Colonel

HER GRANDPARENTS
1915

This film directed by Frank Powell was from another story suggested by a newspaper clipping.

OUT OF BONDAGE   1915

William Hinckley

HER MOTHER'S DAUGHTER
1915

This film was sometimes called "The Nun" and it gave Dorothy a great change of pace.

The exteriors on location were photographed at the Santa Barbara Mission.

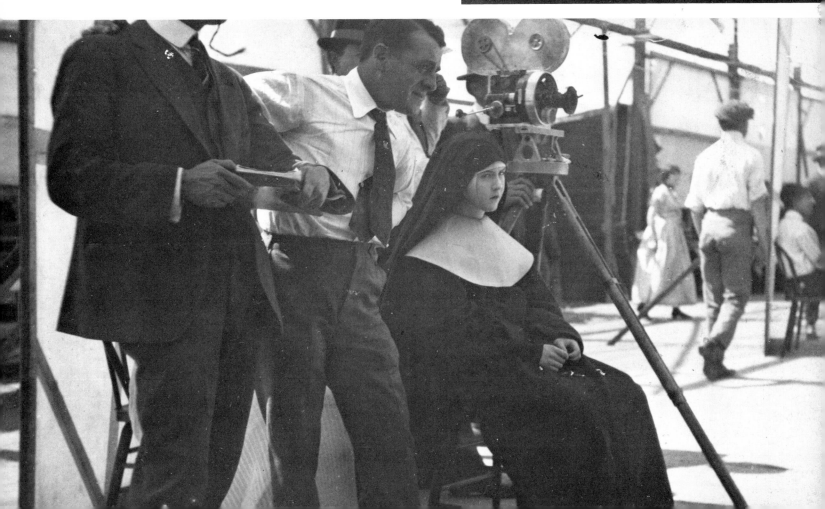

CAPTAIN MACKLIN   1915

A story by Richard Harding Davis

I wore my best dresses in these movies. This is one Madame Frances made for me. It was pink taffeta, black velvet, and ermine. We didn't get paid extra money for wearing our own clothes; we just wanted to look our best.

On the set with Jack Conway in his uniform, Jack Dillon next to him wearing a derby, and Jack O'Brien, the director, sitting next to me. From my expression I can't tell whether I'm contemplating an upcoming scene or plotting a way to get a second dish of ice cream.

My coat I copied from one belonging to my friend Nell Dorr.

ENOCH ARDEN   1915

Acting in silent films took absolute concentration, not easy in studios making many pictures. All of our sets were out of doors, one next to another. No one was closed in, even for the most intimate scenes. You had an audience constantly passing by or standing there watching. The carpenters might be building their set on one side and on the other a director with his megaphone would be yelling so his actors could hear him above the noise while you were trying to play a tender love or sad death scene.

The man on the next set is far more concerned with his lunch than anything Wally Reid and I are doing.

We worked at the studio every day. When not in make-up, we visited those who were. Here Fay Tincher and Teddy Sampson visit Dorothy and me on our sets.

VICTORINE   1915

Ralph Lewis with Dorothy. He played my father in "The Birth."

JORDAN IS A HARD ROAD   1915

Owen Moore was Mary Pickford's first husband.

Usually everyone was allowed to watch rehearsals for a new film. D. W. would turn to see the reaction of the crew or company and ask opinions. He listened to everyone as he knew their counterparts later would be our paying audience.

W. E. Lawrence

BRED IN THE BONE   1915

D. W. Griffith directing a scene with Dorothy and W. E. Lawrence while Teddy Sampson, Mae Marsh, and Donald Crisp watch. Standing in the background is Andy Reid, the electrician we all liked so much.

The Lily · The Rose

Mary Alden

Mary O'Connor and Wilfred Lucas

STORY OF THE PLAY

THE LILY AND THE ROSE

An interesting play is "The Lily and the Rose," the Fine Arts Film production, in which Lillian Gish stars with Rozsika Dolly. Wilfred Lucas plays the part of the man of affairs and ex-football hero, who marries the Lily (Miss Gish), only to forsake her for a dancer, the Rose (Miss Dolly).

The Lily is first seen in a beautiful Southern home, where she is cared for by her two aunts, typical gentlewomen of former days. Through a fashionable relative, the Lily is introduced to the man whom she marries. He gradually tires of the artless girl and goes to a lively show, where he sees a sensational dancer, the Rose. In his infatuation he neglects the Lily. She is unsuspecting until she receives an anonymous warning. Then she tries to win back her husband by giving a new dance that she has learned at a social affair, but he does not give her any encouragement. Then the ways of the husband and wife part. He takes the dancer to the seashore, while the Lily returns to her girlhood home. The man finds that the dancer is shallow and fickle. When he is ready to leave her in disgust he gets a letter from his wife, saying that she had decided that as he was unwilling to be bound by marital ties she had started proceedings for their separation. He goes out to the garden house and shoots himself. The dancer finds him dead and, thinking only of herself, carefully leaves, after wiping out her footprints on the sands.

Now that's what I call a plot!

THE LILY AND THE ROSE   1915

Wilfred Lucas played my husband and Rozsika Dolly of Dolly Sisters fame played the Rose.

LEFT. My apologies to Rosie Dolly. This is the only photograph I have.

OLD HEIDELBERG 1915

During rehearsals Dorothy did not kiss the Prince, Wallace Reid. When it came time for filming she still refused to kiss him. John Emerson, the director from New York as well as the husband of our darling, Anita Loos, asked why. Dorothy naively retorted, "Mr. Emerson, we do not kiss actors. We might catch the Chinese gongo." John informed her that she would indeed kiss Wally and not fake it. Dorothy rushed to Frank "Daddy" Woods, who solved all our problems, and he solved this one. Mrs. Wallace Reid telephoned to assure Dorothy that it was safe to kiss Wally as he was not diseased. The result: Dorothy kissed him.

Raymond Wells and Wallace Reid

We called Anita Loos "Mrs. Spinoza," suspecting that she had a brain. Lorelei Lee proved us right.

Drugs are not new. Even in our small studio there were addicts. Wallace Reid died from narcotics. Dorothy and I were never aware that there was anything wrong with Wally when we worked with him.

BETTY OF GREYSTONE   1916

Film companies had their choice of Florida or California in the winter. Due to the greater variety of scenery, California won out.

Kate Bruce

DAPHNE AND THE PIRATE
1916

Like the majority of his films, Griffith wrote this under a pseudonym. He felt that if the public thought you could do everything, they wouldn't like you.

SOLD FOR MARRIAGE   1916

In searching for new ideas we found a piece of early American history concerning a slave ship full of white women landing in the South. I played a Russian girl brought over to ease the female shortage which had reached the starvation point. The girls were sold for any purpose. Ours was the drama of being "sold for marriage," a small section of the past that our people of today have inherited.

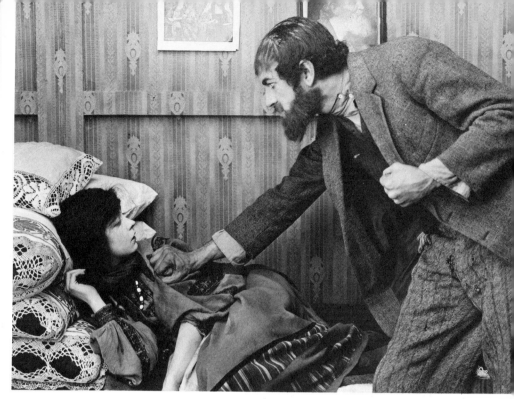

A. D. Sears

Frank Bennett

Walter Long on horseback

LITTLE MEENA'S ROMANCE
1916

Mr. Griffith once heard one of his actresses call a film a "flicker." He told her never to use that word. She was working in the universal language that had been predicted in the Bible, which was to make all men brothers because they would understand each other. This could end wars and bring about the millennium. We were all to remember that the next time we faced a camera.

DOROTHY GISH IN "LITTLE MEENA'S ROMANCE" TRIANGLE PLAYS ©

Fred A. Turner

Kate Toncray   Marguerite Marsh

Owen Moore

SUSAN ROCKS THE BOAT   1916

We remember the times we burst into tears longer than our rare bursts of uncontrolled laughter. The tragedienne has been placed above the comedienne. In the history of entertainment there are many great dramatic talents compared to the few rare comic ones.

INTOLERANCE   1916

The problem of photographing this nearly mile-long set was to be solved by placing the camera in a balloon, but the wind refused to take direction from Mr. Griffith. It would not allow Billy Bitzer to stay steadily within the confines of the high set. Next D. W. put the camera on a rope-manipulated elevator with a tiny platform just large enough to hold himself, Billy, and me, sitting under the camera with my feet hanging over. He had "Huck" Wortman lay small tracks to put it on, leading into the set with three thousand people. As the men pushed the little elevator forward, they slowly lowered it. Thus the first crane shot was born.

The eagle eye of Bitzer kept everything in focus, even the people you see on top of the wall three-quarters of a mile away. The unbroken scene lasted several minutes, going over the heads of the Denishawn dancing girls, with three bands playing simultaneously, down to the banquet table with the King at one end and his Princess at the other. It ended on two white doves pulling a miniature golden chariot with a white rose in it for his Beloved.

This unbelievably beautiful shot has been cut up and lost forever.

"Intolerance" was Mr. Griffith's monument. "Think as I think or be damned!" was the theme.

The film contained four complete stories: the fall of Babylon, the Crucifixion, the St. Bartholomew's Day massacre in France, and the battle between capital and labor in America at the beginning of the twentieth century. The original version was to run eight hours in length, seen on two separate occasions with a dinner intermission between. "Intolerance" was fifty or a hundred years ahead of its time. Griffith, unfortunately, listened to the exhibitors, who earlier had refused to run "The Birth of the Nation" at its length. He proved "The Birth's" value by putting it first into legitimate theatres, but even with its success they still would not hear of a longer film and "Intolerance" was mutilated. Today there is not in existence the complete version of this classic.

The entire construction crew from "Intolerance," very tired when this was taken. This photograph was sent me by Mrs. M. A. Cotter of Hoodsport, Washington, whose father, Hal Sullivan (second row on the right, with his elbow out), was our assistant property and special effects man. Ralph de Lacy (front row right with hat, and hands in pockets) was our head property man. "Huck" Wortman, our genius carpenter, is in the front row with the hat and open vest. Jim Newman, the assistant carpenter, is behind "Huck" to his right with the cocked hat, and Shorty English, our carpenter, is in the front row turned sideways, with the spot in the center of his overalls.

This is from the modern section of the film. On the set are Billy Bitzer, in the straw hat with his back turned, "Huck" Wortman, pushing the wheelbarrow, Seena Owen (The Princess Beloved) with the parasol, and D. W. in the Chinese hat.

D. W. Griffith conceived and created *every aspect of this film—story, sets, costumes—even down to the first false eyelashes for the Princess Beloved. They were made on the set by the man in charge of beards for the extras.*

"Huck" Wortman, Mr. Griffith, and Billy Bitzer spent hours on the vacant lot discussing where to build, so that the sun would be in a certain place at the right time of the year to give the proper lighting when the various scenes would be photographed.

An ambulance, nurse, and doctor were kept available during the building as well as the filming in case of accidents, but they were never needed.

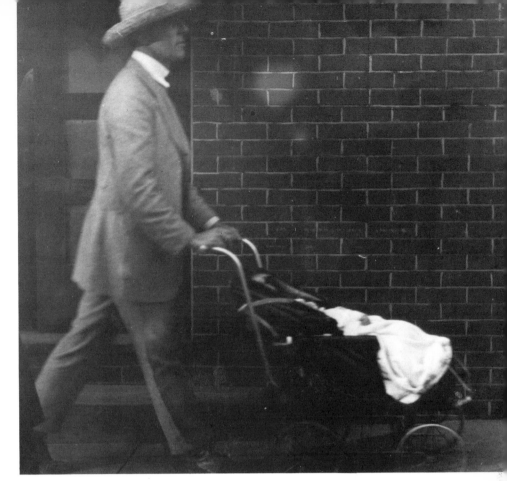

D. W. Griffith playing the part of a proud mother

Griffith used Walt Whitman's words, "Out of the cradle endlessly rocking," to tie his four stories together. My part for these flashes, shown here, took less than an hour to film.

THE LITTLE SCHOOL MA'AM
1916

Elmer Clifton played opposite Dorothy. He later became a famous director and discovered Clara Bow.

The Franklin brothers, Charles M. and Sidney A., were co-directors on this film. Both had long and distinguished careers.

We always applied our own make-up. Douglas Fairbanks created the make-up man. He thought it too feminine to use a powder-puff so he had a barber's chair installed in his dressing room and trained a man to make him up.

Elmer Clifton

Photograph by Charles Albin

DIANE OF THE FOLLIES   1916

Virgins are the hardest roles to play. Those dear little girls—to make them interesting takes great vitality, but a fallen woman or a vamp!—75 per cent of your work is already done.

PATHWAYS OF LIFE   1916

W. E. Lawrence and Spottiswoode Aitken

LOWER LEFT. Olga Grey is the handsome woman wearing earrings.

ATTA BOY'S LAST RACE   1916

When we knew the plot of our silent films, we rehearsed them saying to each other whatever came into our minds that seemed to fit the action. Often it was so right that our words later became the subtitles.

CHILDREN OF THE FEUD   1916

Sam DeGrasse

THE CHILDREN PAY
1916

That's Alma Rubens in the middle with
Billy Bitzer's niece, Maizie Radford, who
later married Guy Bolton. He wrote the
"book" for "Anya."

The heavy-set lady is Jennie
Lee in white face. Earlier
she had played in "The Birth"
in black face.

Violet Wilkie

Ralph Lewis pounding the
table to make a point.
Seated is Mary O'Connor.

THE LITTLE YANK
1917

Alberta Lee, who played Mrs. Abraham Lincoln in "The Birth of a Nation."

Jack Brammall

THE HOUSE BUILT
UPON SAND
1917

The lad in the cap (to my right), our cousin, Clay McConnell, played in this film.

Jennie Lee from "The Birth" again playing in black face

Spottiswoode Aitken

SOULS TRIUMPHANT 1917

Unidentified actress, Kate Bruce, and William "Christy" Cabanne, one of my directors who was visiting on the set

FINE ARTS—GRIFFITH STARS

BACK ROW: Dorothy Gish, Seena Owen, Norma Talmadge. MIDDLE ROW: Robert (Bobby) Harron, Harry Aitken (producer), Sir Beerbohm-Tree, Owen Moore, Wilfred Lucas. FRONT ROW: Douglas Fairbanks, Bessie Love, Constance Talmadge, Constance Collier, Lillian Gish, Fay Tincher, DeWolfe Hopper.

Photograph courtesy of Raymond Lee of Roy George Assoc.

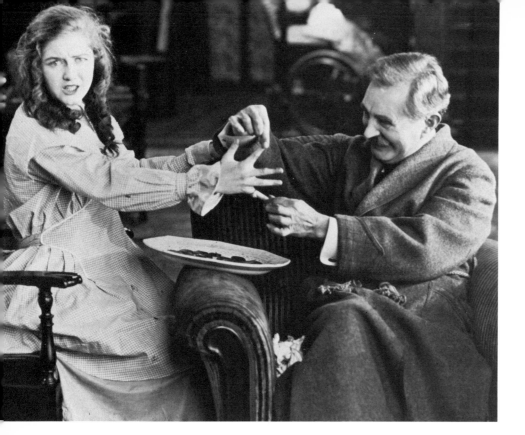

HEARTS OF THE WORLD
1918

While D. W. was in Britain in early 1917 for the opening of "The Birth of a Nation" and "Intolerance," the first films to be shown at the Drury Lane Theatre in London, he was invited to 10 Downing Street to see the Prime Minister. Lloyd George asked Mr. Griffith to produce a film for the English and French governments to persuade America to go to war. D. W. sent for his cameraman and three players to join him. Mother and I sailed in March on the "St. Louis." Dorothy, Bobby Harron, and Billy Bitzer sailed with General Pershing on the "Baltic" soon after.

D. W. rehearsed us in the twelve-reel "Hearts of the World" as well as in the seven-reel "The Great Love" and the six-reel "The Greatest Thing in Life." We filmed some exteriors in England. We were sent to the front where trained nurses were not allowed because they were too valuable. Mr. Griffith was forced to use an Army cameraman because Wilhelm Gottlieb Bitzer was not allowed into France. We came home with eighty-six thousand feet of film in October and rushed to Hollywood where the company was waiting so we could complete our three films quickly. We

worked day and night through the holidays and it was Twelfth-night before we could enjoy the tree and presents Mother had placed underneath.

As a result of this film the noted historian Dr. Francis Trevelyan Miller wrote Mr. Griffith the following:

"It may interest you to know that we the Board of Historians agree that your production of 'Hearts of the World' is the most notable on record that the war has produced.

I have written nineteen volumes on the war. But in one single picture, you produce a vital, human record that embodies the spirit and soul of the war with deeper reality than all these books combined.

I have come to the conclusion that hereafter history must be divided into four epochs: the stone age, the bronze age, the age of the printed page—and the film age—of which you, Mr. Griffith, are the first of the great cinema historians.

This is the position that you will occupy in the records of human progress."

"HEARTS OF THE WORLD"

D. W. GRIFFITH'S
SUPREME TRIUMPH

A Romance of the Great War
THE SWEETEST LOVE
STORY EVER TOLD

OVER THERE
1918

"KILL ME, DEAREST, RATHER
THAN LET THE GERMANS
CAPTURE ME ALIVE"

FACING DEATH,
THE GERMAN OFFICER'S
WOOING

MURDER **RUIN**

BATTLE SCENES
TAKEN ON
THE BATTLE FIELDS
OF FRANCE

WITH
LILLIAN GISH
DOROTHY GISH
AND ROBERT HARRON

BROADWAY
THEATRE
Copyright Key Publishing Co.

NOW PLAYING—TWICE DAILY

Daily Matinees 25c to $1.00
Eves. & Sat. Mat. 25c to $1.50

Noel Coward

While our little group of six was living in Broadway, England, filming scenes for "Hearts," we were joined by a lad who was to play several roles in the picture. This was his film debut and he later told us that Mother took him into our midst and made him feel like one of the family. After Mother became an invalid this very busy man always found time to pay her a visit on his trips to America. Tenderness was one of the least exploited qualities of Sir Noel.

Mr. Griffith at the front in 1917

Dorothy was so amusing as "The Little Disturber" that Paramount signed her to star in her own comedies: The Dorothy Gish Artcraft Series.

Little Ben Alexander long before "Dragnet" fame

BATTLING JANE 1918

Obviously Dorothy threw herself into the title role with great enthusiasm.

Courtesy Paramount-Artcraft

Mother never attended business meetings with us. When Paramount offered Dorothy, who was still in her teens, a million dollars for a series of five-reel comedies, she refused. We asked her why. She said, "At my age all that money would ruin my character."

OUT OF LUCK 1919

Dorothy discovered Rudolph Valentino dancing in a nightclub. Mr. Griffith's film, "Scarlet Days," called for a Spanish hero, but D. W. turned Dorothy down, saying, "He's too foreign looking. The girls would never like him." Dorothy knew better. We used to go horseback riding on Sundays and Rudy would come back to the house and cook a big spaghetti supper. He designed our riding habits for us which have been given to the Museum of the City of New York. When Dorothy used him in "Out of Luck" she discovered he was so fastidious that it took him too long to dress and he held up their shooting schedule. Rudy originally came to America to be a landscape architect.

Courtesy Paramount-Artcraft

Photograph courtesy of Raymond Lee of Roy George Assoc.

THE GREATEST THING IN LIFE   1918

This film was Griffith's answer to those who thought he did not like black people. He wrote a story of a white snob who fancied himself better than others. The story ended in a shell hole with bombs bursting near by. The snob is with a dying black man who in his delirium thinks the white man is his mother. He takes him in his arms and when he asks his "Mammy" to kiss the pain away, the white man kisses him full on the lips—and holds it. The audience sat tense and wept. A daring scene to film even today. It is a pity that this picture has been destroyed or lost.

This rare still from "The Greatest Thing in Life" is with David Butler, who later became a famous director.

A ROMANCE OF HAPPY VALLEY
1919

This film was lost to our world until Russia presented a beautiful print to the Museum of Modern Art in 1971. They ran the original copy with Russian subtitles. My Russian startled me.

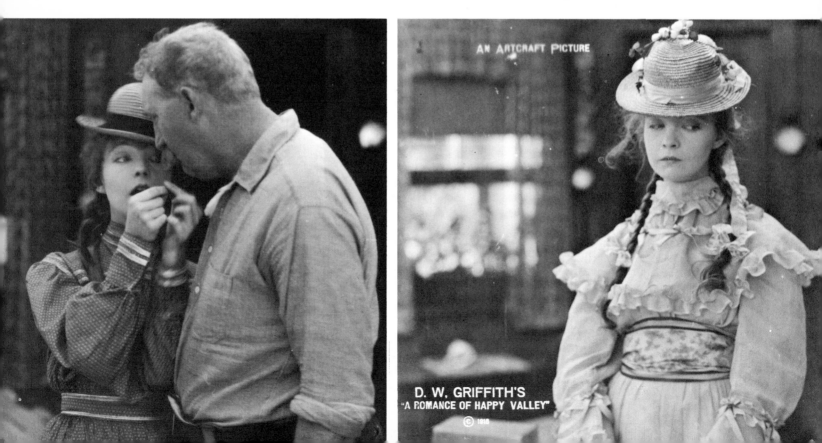

AN ARTCRAFT PICTURE

D. W. GRIFFITH'S
"A ROMANCE OF HAPPY VALLEY"

PEPPY POLLY   1919

One of Dorothy's Paramount Artcraft Series in which she played a hoyden in trouble with the law. She was befriended by a young physician portrayed by Richard Barthelmess. Naturally in the story she falls in love with him.

Courtesy Paramount-Artcraft

Richard Barthelmess and Josephine Crowell

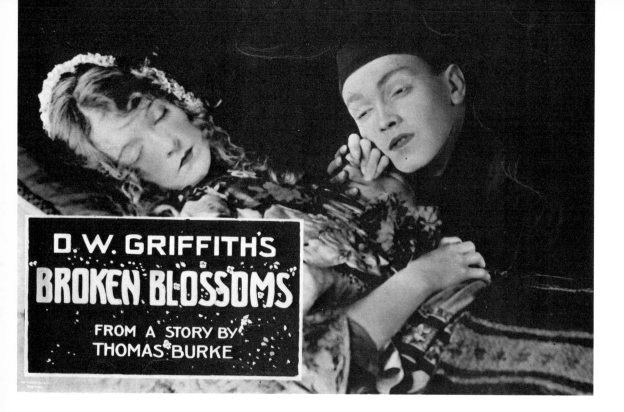

BROKEN BLOSSOMS   1919

It took eighteen days and nights to complete "Broken Blossoms." There were no retakes or

added scenes. It had been timed so perfectly in rehearsals that when the film was run for the first time it was only two hundred feet (less than three minutes) over length, which meant that after snipping off the beginning

Richard Barthelmess and Donald Crisp

and the end of each scene it was ready for the musical score. If you want to save money making a film, this is the way to do it.

It ran less than ninety minutes but opened in a Broadway theatre at three dollars a seat, top prices for any play at that time. One critic said its perfection should make it the bible at the right hand of every director of the future.

The only difference of opinion between D. W. Griffith and me was how to play young. I felt he wanted me to imitate a victim of St. Vitus dance. His answer was, "How am I to get contrast between the old and the young?" I had my way once, in the playing of the child in "Broken Blossoms."

NUGGET NELL   1919

Dorothy's great Western satire

Courtesy Paramount-Artcraft

Raymond D. Cannon

"We do right by our men and drink our whiskey straight."

TRUE HEART SUSIE   1919

Griffith took the Dora Agnes story from "David Copperfield," set it in New England in the early part of this century, and called it "True Heart Susie." This rural poem has become a classic. It was Queen Mother Alexandria's favorite film and she kept a print of it at Buckingham Palace.

All leading men were called "John"—all leading ladies became "Mary"—here with "Mary"—the cow

THE GREATEST QUESTION   1919

I'LL GET HIM YET   1919

Courtesy Paramount-Artcraft

Ralph Graves

Porter Strong, Ed Peil, Ralph Graves, and Richard Barthelmess

George Fawcett

Richard Barthelmess' mother coached the great Russian actress, Nazimova, with her English. Later Madame Nazimova gave Dick a small part in "War Brides" which Dorothy saw. She persuaded Mr. Griffith to bring him to Hollywood to be her leading man, and later on I got him—for two pictures, "Broken Blossoms" and "Way Down East."

Richard Barthelmess

She got him!

Our first car we bought second hand from Jack Pickford. We were so proud of it that the three of us quickly learned to drive. Dorothy became the expert.

With Mother

OPPOSITE. Richard Barthelmess with Lillian and Dorothy
Photograph by James Abbe

Me, Mary Alden, Dorothy, Constance Talmadge and Mildred Harris

SECOND DECADE

*C*ELEBRATION was the spirit of the twenties. Radio hit the country with a bang. Amos 'n Andy's air time changed train schedules. Prohibition brought in the speakeasies. One rarely lunched or dined far from a dance floor. The Charleston and *the dansants* were the vogue. Eugene O'Neill gave us his first full-length play. Great movie theatres thrived, some held over six thousand people. They also presented one-hundred-piece orchestras, teaching a new public to listen to symphonic music. Charles Lindbergh became the world's hero. Films divorced music and married English words. Everyone was playing the market. The crash in late October of '29 again changed our lives.

MARY ELLEN COMES TO TOWN
1920

Dorothy was directed by Elmer Clifton, who played my elder brother in "The Birth of a Nation."

Courtesy Paramount-Artcraft

REMODELING HER HUSBAND
1920

With James Rennie. Directed by Lillian Gish

While the studio was being built in Mamaroneck, Mr. Griffith was rehearsing two stories to be made in Florida. He needed all the crew and wanted Dorothy's director, Elmer Clifton, to help him. To my amazement he asked me to direct her next film for Paramount. He flattered me by telling me I knew as much about making pictures as he did and more about acting. I thought he was teasing me until he gave the same story to the press.

Dorothy showed us a cartoon of a husband complaining that his wife was so dowdy no man ever glanced at her. She angrily tells him to follow her down Fifth Avenue and she will show him. As he walks in back of her she makes an ugly or pretty face at every man she passes so of course they turn around. (Later this same scene was used by Judy Garland and Fred Astaire in "Easter Parade.") We quickly wrote a five-reel story around this, cast and rehearsed for D. W. as he was leaving for the South. I picked the furniture, told "Huck" Wortman how to do the sets, saw to the costumes (we had no designers then), and was given fifty thousand dollars to make the film.

It was November and cold. The studio had no heat or lights. I had to put extra strong telegraph poles all the way out to Orienta Point because the wiring was so heavy. Getting the heat for such an enormous building took so long I had to rent a small New Rochelle studio, move our sets and furniture, and start working there.

When Griffith returned I asked him why he left me to direct my first film along with the chaos of building a studio. He laughed and said, "I knew the men would work harder and faster for a girl. I'm no fool."

Dorothy began having ideas different from mine, so I started taking a scene her way, then mine, so we could judge when we saw it on the screen. This was expensive so I rehearsed her love scenes longer than necessary as she seemed very interested in James Rennie. She married him a year later.

Dorothy with her future
husband James Rennie

"Remodeling" was the only picture I ever directed.
Later I directed John Gay's "The Beggar's Opera"
in New Orleans.

**WAY DOWN EAST
1920**

George Neville (Reuben Whipple), Edgar Nelson (Hi Holler), Burr McIntosh (Squire Bartlett), Kate Bruce (Mrs. Bartlett), Richard Barthelmess (David Bartlett), Lillian Gish (Anna Moore), Lowell Sherman (Lennox Sanderson), Vivia Ogden (Martha Perkins), Creighton Hale (Professor Sterling), Mary Hay (Kate Brewster), and Porter Strong (Seth Holcomb)

Just as "Uncle Tom's Cabin" influenced the middle of the nineteenth century, "Way Down East's" appeal in the theatre lasted nearly twenty-five years as we entered the twentieth century.

The butler almost refuses Anna Moore entrance.

My dressing gown and this timeless, classic ballgown (below) were created at Henri Bendel's shop on West Fifty-seventh Street in New York City.

Lowell Sherman as Lennox Sanderson

Patricia Fruen and Mrs. Morgan Belmont. Mrs. Belmont, one of the leading society women of New York, was cast because of her look of distinction. Griffith also raided the Ziegfeld Follies for the beauties in the party scene.

Florence Short as the Eccentric Aunt

Josephine Bernard (Mrs. Tremont), Patricia Fruen (Sister), and Mrs. Morgan Belmont (Diana Tremont)

Anna Moore tricked by the mock marriage. The man in the derby is not an actor but our assistant director, Herbert Sutch. In those days you worked wherever needed.

We rehearsed ten hours a day for eight weeks, with Billy Bitzer and his stop watch clocking each scene down to the shortest flash. Our story went before the camera with the timing and changing tempo of a finished symphony.

Burr McIntosh (Squire Bartlett) will have none of Anna's pleading. With Richard Barthelmess.

Richard Barthelmess as David Bartlett
with his mother played by Kate Bruce

Burr McIntosh was a dear man and a very good actor. Mr. Griffith
could not understand why he wouldn't be stern enough when he
had to turn me out into the blizzard. Little did he know that the
Burr McIntosh magazine hired two little girls to pose for five
dollars each a day. (See the photograph with the deer in "The
Beginning.")

Emily Fitzroy (Maria Poole) tells Vivia
Ogden (Martha Perkins) the secret of
Anna Moore's illegitimate baby. Griffith
used a staccato tempo for Vivia as the
local gossip.

*Griffith always gave special lighting to
his character people so they would look
beautiful, particularly his mothers.
"Brucie" became an adopted member
of the Gish family. We always wondered how and why she ever got into
the world of theatre and films. She
belonged in a convent.*

*The two beautiful photographs with
Kate Bruce are by James Abbe.*

The filming of the barn dance sequence in which Norma Shearer appeared as an extra

Discussing a scene with D. W. Griffith

OPPOSITE, UPPER RIGHT
With Mr. Griffith on location waiting for a set-up

OPPOSITE, RIGHT
White River Junction, Vermont

Being "launched" by the crew

We lost several members of our crew from pneumonia as the result of exposure. Clarine Seymour died ten days after we worked in a blizzard throughout the night. She was replaced by an actress of the same size; the blizzard had ended and her scenes could not be redone. Mary Hay, who replaced Clarine, became the first Mrs. Richard Barthelmess a year later.

Mr. Griffith built a tiny bridge out over the falls just strong enough to hold himself, Billy Bitzer, and the camera.

D. W. Griffith

Being rescued by Richard Barthelmess. Years later when we saw this film, Dick said, "There isn't enough money in the world to make me do that again."

THE HISTORY OF "WAY DOWN EAST"

"Way Down East," by Lottie Blair Parker, was first produced as a stage play in 1896 under the title of "Annie Laurie." A tour of New England revealed the fact that certain alterations in the play's construction were needed, and it was temporarily withdrawn by its producer, William A. Brady.

Mr. Brady's partner, Joseph R. Grismer, elaborated the work of Miss Parker, and the play in its new form and re-named "Way Down East" was shown within a few months at the old Schiller Theatre (now the Garrick) in Chicago.

At the conclusion of a sensational success in Chicago, "Way Down East" was brought to New York in February 1898 and presented at the Manhattan Theatre, Sixth Avenue and Thirty-third Street, then under the direction of William A. Brady and Florenz Ziegfeld, Jr. Within a few days it became the talk of New York and remained at the Manhattan Theatre for seven months, at that time considered a phenomenal run.

There were many gala performances during the New York engagement, not the least among them that of Monday evening, April 18, 1898, when President and Mrs. William McKinley occupied a box.

In the cast of "Way Down East" on the evening when the President and his party saw the play were Burr McIntosh, Mrs. Sara Stevens, Howard Kyle, Louise Galloway, George Backus, Felix Haney, Phoebe Davies, Frank Lander, Vivia Ogden, Charles V. Seamon, John Bunny, and J. H. Davies.

For twenty-two years "Way Down East" has been a classic of the American theatre, presented from coast to coast in every city and town large enough to boast a theatre or a town hall.

(From the 1920 film souvenir book)

A grave near the Boston Common where all illegitimate children were buried when they died.

(Photograph by Richard W. Sears)

The happy ending

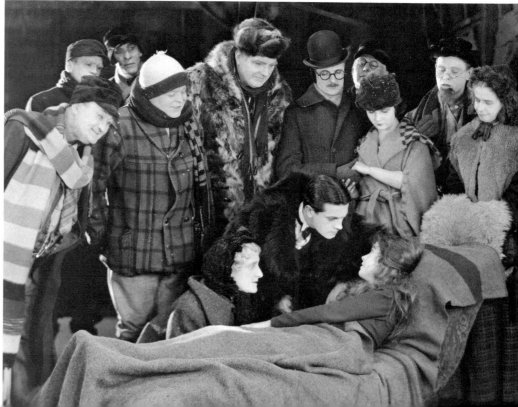

Dorothy   *Photograph by Kenneth Alexander*

Lillian   *Photograph by Preston Duncan*

Lillian, Mother, Dorothy on the Santa Fe Limited

FLYING PAT   1920

Courtesy Paramount-Artcraft

At this time one of the requisites of pilot training was to be strapped into a chair that rotated, turning the occupant upside down, revolving all the time. This sequence was used in the film with many hilarious close-ups of Dorothy upside down staring into the camera in utter confusion. The only problem with shooting this portion of "Flying Pat" was that Dorothy promptly became air sick. She was a Pisces and always preferred the sea to the sky.

Harold Vizard and James Rennie

ORPHANS OF THE STORM
1922

*When rehearsals began on "Orphans"
Dorothy decided on the part of the
blind Louise. Every spare moment was
spent reading about the world at the
end of the eighteenth century, especially the French revolution. (Carlyle's
book was in everyone's pocket.) When
the Royalists rioted in front of the
theatre in Paris when the film opened
there, Griffith used his source of information as his defense.*

Morgan Wallace

*Our two sixteen-year-old cousins, Dor-
othy McConnell and Ruth Cleaver,
are on the right in this picture. I
dressed them in the style of Gains-
borough and Greuze. The costumes
were so heavy Dorothy fainted before
the long day was over. They both decided films were too hard and happily
became Mrs. Joseph Davis of Dayton,
Ohio, and Mrs. Ted Seith of San Jose,
California.*

Joseph Schildkraut and Morgan Wallace

Dorothy as the blind Louise

Joseph Schildkraut

Frank Puglia, Lucille LaVerne, Dorothy, and Sheldon Lewis

Frank Puglia, whom we found on Fourteenth Street,
in the Italian company of "Two Orphans"

Lucille LaVerne

Monte Blue as Danton and Sidney Herbert as Robespierre

For the big scene around the guillotine we chose a Sunday to film so the residents of the town were glad to take part. It was like a picnic for them since they were each given lunch and a dollar twenty-five for the day. How Mr. Griffith managed to make so many look French and hungry at the same time I will never know.

We had photographs of old Paris streets which our genius carpenter, "Huck" Wortman, built on the lot at our studio in Mamaroneck.

Frank "Huck" Wortman

Leslie King

BENEFIT FOR DESTITUTE RUSSIAN
ARTISTS GIVEN BY
BALIEFF'S "CHAUVE-SOURIS"
SUNDAY EVENING, APRIL 9TH, 1922
WITH THE ENDORSEMENT OF THE
AMERICAN RELIEF ADMINISTRATION

WITH YOUR GREAT ASSISTANCE—

LILLIAN GISH
IN REMEMBRANCE OF A NIGHT NEVER TO BE
FORGOTTEN, AND THAT YOU HELPED MAKE POS-
SIBLE WITH YOUR WONDERFUL SPIRIT IN AS-
SISTING THESE THOUSAND AND ONE HUNGRY
SOULS IN RUSSIA.
MORRIS GEST

Balieff, Sam Bernard, Leon Errol, Marilyn Miller, Walter Catlett, Laurette Taylor, Al Jolson, Doris Keane, Lenore Ulric, the Gish Girls, Morris Gest, and Ed Wynn

Benefit for destitute Russian arts given by Balieff's "Chauve-Souris" Sunday evening, April 9, 1922, with the endorsement of the American Relief Administration. The inscription from Morris Gest reads, "With your great assistance—In remembrance of a night never to be forgotten. And that you helped make possible with your wonderful spirit in assisting these thousand and one hungry souls in Russia."

FURY   1923

Henry King directed "Fury" before he left for Italy to direct "The White Sister."

Richard Barthelmess

THE WHITE SISTER   1923

With Ronald Colman in his first major role

Religious stories from the Bible were accepted by the exhibitors but this was the first modern story based on Catholicism. We made it independently and could not get a release for it. The big companies who owned the theatres said the public could get religion free on Sundays, they're not going to pay for it during the week. When they refused to let us play in movie theatres, we opened at the George M. Cohan Theatre in New York. The film was an instant success and Nick Schenck, head of MGM, released it. A year later Metro offered me their highest-paid contract.

James Abbe was New York's most sought after photographer with a studio on Fifth Avenue bringing in several thousand dollars a month. He gave it all up to go to Italy with us on "The White Sister" for a hundred and fifty dollars a week.

OVERLEAF. Lillian and Ronald Colman

All "The White Sister" photographs are by James Abbe.

Juliette La Violette, a French actress, played Madame Bernard, my chaperone in the film. Mrs. George (Pettie) Kratsch, who lived down the street from our Aunt Emily in Massillon, Ohio, was my chaperone in real life.

This story allowed us to photograph a wedding that had never been filmed—the bride in all her finery being married to the church. It always took place just before dawn.

At F. Marion Crawford's villa in Sorrento
with director Henry King

We were the first Americans to arrive in Italy
to make a film. Instead of a studio we found
an empty building with two klieg lights. The
only place near we could get the equipment
that we needed was Germany.

Our story had, I thought, an impossible situation for a successful film. The man the girl
is to marry is sent to war. Word comes that he
has been killed, the girl enters a convent and
we see her taking her final vows. Then the
lover returns, hears of it, goes to the convent,
and kidnaps her. They go to another country
and are married. You can't care about a character you see taking solemn vows before God
at eight o'clock and then by nine o'clock
changing her mind. We decided we would
have to kill one of them. Since the nun's life
was secure, we killed Ronnie.

Photograph by
Charles Albin

THE BRIGHT SHAWL
1923

"The Bright Shawl" was based on a novelette by Joseph Hergesheimer who was one of the most highly acclaimed fiction writers of this period. Dorothy played "La Cavel," a Cuban dancer, who was entranced by Richard Barthelmess. Dick persuaded her to work with him to gain information for the rebels against the Spanish army. She paid for her deception with her life, dying in the arms of Barthelmess. The exteriors were filmed in Havana and the cast included William Powell, Mary Astor, Edward G. Robinson, Jetta Goudal, and André de Beranger.

Richard Barthelmess

OPPOSITE. Photograph by Charles Albin

William Powell on the sofa

Film stars honored by Cuban Republic.
Miss Dorothy Gish carrying a twenty-five-thousand-dollar Cuban shawl and Mr. Richard Barthelmess holding a thousand-dollar gold mounted Malacca cane presented by General M. Betancourt of the Cuban army and Felipe Taboada, Counsel General of Cuba, on behalf of the Cuban nation for their portrayal of Cuba's struggle for independence in the new motion picture "The Bright Shawl." General Betancourt, Miss Gish, Mr. Barthelmess, John S. Robertson, who directed the picture, and Counsul General Taboada.

ROMOLA   1924

Georges Clemenceau, former Premier of France: "Such a work of art merits every success."

Giavonni Poggi, Resident Director of the Uffizi Gallery, Florence, and curator of all the royal galleries of Tuscany: "In 'Romola' the physical aspects of Florence, as it existed in the fifteenth century, are faithfully reproduced."

Firmin Gemier, Director of the Odéon National Theatre, Paris: "Your reconstruction of the golden age of Florence gave me one of the greatest surprises of my life."

William Powell as Tito Melema, the most interesting character in the story— the villain.

OPPOSITE, TOP.
The burning of Savonarola on the cross

OPPOSITE, BOTTOM.
Romola with Tessa's child

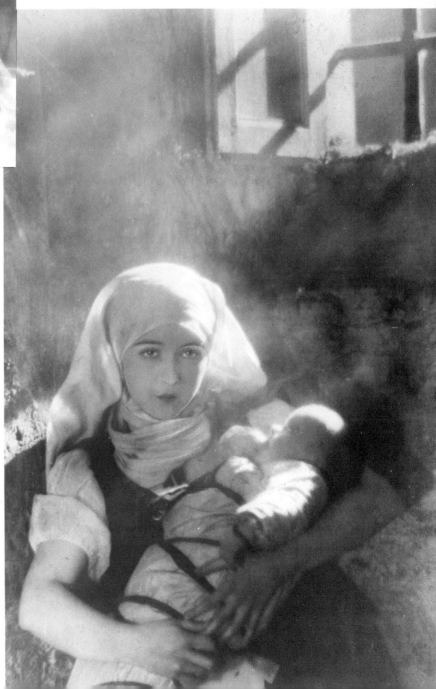

Tessa with her illegitimate baby by Tito Melema

Romola with Carlo (Ronald Colman), Savonarola (Herbert Grimwood), and Romola's father, Bardo Bardi (Bonaventura Ibanez)

OPPOSITE. The library with Ronald Colman

Dorothy as Tessa in her kitchen

Charles Albin who took these magnificent stills. An unfrocked Franciscan monk, he later returned to the monastery.

Charles Lane as Tito's father, Baldassare Calve. He was six feet, three inches, with great distinction and beauty that cannot be concealed, even in rags.

Dr. Guida Biagi, Director of the Laurentian Library, Florence: "It has the authenticity and atmosphere of the golden age of the Renaissance of which the Florence of the Medici was the center."

Leonce Benedite, Director of the Luxembourg Museum and the Rodin Museum, Paris: "It is notable for its settings, its costumes and its vibrant semblance of reality."

Pierre Bonnard, the French painter: "It will awaken longings for the glorious past and enthuse all souls that follow ideals."

Douglas Fairbanks, Sr.: "The most stunningly beautiful picture in every last detail."

Santiago Alba, former Minister of Arts in Spain: "It is a page of the most delicate art and appeals like few other films."

All other photographs of "Romola" by Charles Albin

Photographs by J. C. Milligan

With Sid Grauman. Even in Lavin's gowns you can still see Dorothy's reaction to Hollywood hoop-la.

THE BEAUTIFUL CITY
1925

An early film of racial strife filmed in the slums of the Lower East Side of New York with Dorothy playing an Irish colleen opposite the Italian Richard Barthelmess

William Powell

Dorothy with William Powell and Richard Barthelmess

Richard Barthelmess

Leon Errol

Dorothy was always anxious to work with expert comedians like Leon Errol. She also was always startled to find them the most worried and serious of men.

Nita Naldi was a famous "vamp" who played opposite Rudolph Valentino in "Blood and Sand."

136

LA BOHÈME   1926

OPPOSITE. John Gilbert
*Photograph by
Kenneth Alexander*

Roy D'Arcy   Mimi.   *Photograph by Ruth Harriet Louise*

Edward Everett Horton,
John Gilbert,
George Hassell,
Gino Corrado,
and Renée Adorée

All production photographs from the MGM release "LA BOHEME" © 1926 Metro-Goldwyn-Mayer Corporation. Copyright renewed 1954 by Loew's Incorporated

Puccini died before we filmed "Bohème." His estate being in litigation we were unable to use his musical score. Two gifted composers, Mendosa and Axt, orchestrated every scene so beautifully that George Jean Nathan said it was better than the original.

Roy D'Arcy

Gino Corrado and Renée Adorée

In 1926 there were twenty-one thousand movie theatres in the United States versus five hundred legitimate houses. In 1927 Paramount opened Grauman's Chinese Theatre in Hollywood with a seating capacity of twenty-five hundred and in 1928 the Roxy opened in New York holding six thousand two hundred and fifty. Their first week at a dollar top price the Roxy grossed a hundred and ten thousand dollars and the first year a total of five and a half million dollars.

John Gilbert

At the ballet in my one Erté costume

It was great news when I heard that "Erté," the French artist, would help with costumes. Being unfamiliar with pictures he would not believe me when I told him worn-out rags of silk would move better and look poorer than new calico at five cents a yard, so with one exception I did my own costumes with the help of Mother Coulter, head of our wardrobe at MGM. Renée Adorée would not follow me and her delicate beauty was smothered by a coarse heavy wig and dresses so gross they hid and killed all movement of her appealing little French body that helped so to make "The Big Parade" a hit.

Photograph by Kenneth Alexander

Karl Dane

Renée Adorée

"La Bohème" was the first picture in Hollywood made entirely with pancromatic film.

King Vidor, our director, is a Texan and a highly talented gentle man.

California ranch. All these people and paraphernalia to take an exterior of the pool. John Gilbert on my right in the overcoat and King Vidor on my left in the dark suit and light hat.

Photograph by Cecil Beaton

Lillian by Helleu

Dorothy by L. J. Malba

THE SCARLET LETTER   1926

Lars Hanson

Joyce Coad

MGM had no story for me. When I told Louis B. Mayer that the problem of an actor to play the Reverend Dimsdale had kept me from doing "The Scarlet Letter" he ran "The Story of Gosta Berling" for me. I rushed back to his office to tell him how perfect the actor, Lars Hanson, was and asked if I might do it with him as my second picture for them. He said "no" it was on the blacklist. An American classic taught in our schools? Why? I wrote to the Women's Clubs, churches, etc., objecting. They answered and said if I would take full responsibility they would lift the ban. Mr. Mayer sent to Sweden for Lars Hanson, let me have Victor Seastrom, the great Swedish artist, as director and put it into my hands. I worked with Frances Marion on the script and we made a successful film that is regarded as a classic to this day.

When Lars Hanson arrived from Sweden he could not speak a word of English; all our scenes were played by us in our native tongues. Seastrom, our director, who spoke both languages, was amazed when we understood each other exactly in our scenes together. It is always a thrill to play with a fine and true professional—in any language.

Karl Dane

Not having seen Henry Walthall in nearly ten years I asked for him to play the husband. When we met I was a head taller. He had to play our scenes together standing on wooden boxes.

Henry B. Walthall

OPPOSITE. *Photograph by Ruth Harriet Louise*

Victor Seastrom in the white shirt wearing a cap directing a scene with Joyce Coad and myself

OPPOSITE: *Photograph by Hayningen-Huene, Vogue Studio Paris*

Musicians, cast, and crew on location. I had worked twelve years in films where there was never music on the set. To my surprise, at MGM the company could not act without it. To me it was a distraction but I was outnumbered.

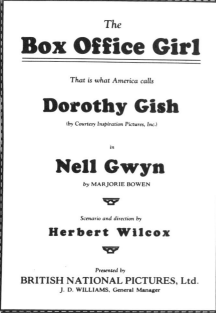

The
Box Office Girl

That is what America calls

Dorothy Gish

(by Courtesy Inspiration Pictures, Inc.)

in

Nell Gwyn

by MARJORIE BOWEN

✦

Scenario and direction by

Herbert Wilcox

✦

Presented by

BRITISH NATIONAL PICTURES, Ltd.
J. D. WILLIAMS, General Manager

NELL GWYN   1926

A Dorothy Gish Success In "Nell Gwyn."

The presence of Dorothy Gish in this British film has enabled it to secure a footing in America, and it must be said that she is the life and soul of the piece, Herbert Wilcox, the director, having made skilful use of her comedienne's talent and daring use of her considerable physical attractions.

This English screen production of "Nell Gwyn" is going to lead a great many people to believe that they have discovered a new Dorothy Gish. But she is the same Dorothy Gish as always, but here at last has come a part that gives this consummate screen player a chance to really show what she can do.

But it is to Dorothy Gish that the greatest tribute should be paid. Superb isn't the word that fits her performance; tremendous would possibly more actually convey the work she does. She is at once Gish, Pickford, Negri and Swanson in one.

Star, March 2

NELL COMES TO LIFE

Delightful Qualities in New British-Made Film

Dorothy Gish.—The Nell Gwyn of Dorothy Gish is perfectly delightful. Her moods range from low comedy to high tragedy. She passes from one emotion to another naturally and logically. She makes Nell a living, vibrant personality. This is by far the best work she has ever done.

Sunday Pictorial, March 7

British Films Triumph

The Plaza Theatre, the magnificent new picture house at Piccadilly Circus, has behind it one of the greatest American film-producing concerns. That this elegant temple of the cinema should open its doors with a British film as the star attraction was something more than a diplomatic concession to the demand for British films. It was a well-deserved American compliment to a very fine British photoplay. Mr Herbert Wilis's film, "Nell Gwyn," proved itself worthy of the honour. Here we have a photoplay that tells a straightforward story with artistry and without those extravagances that so often mar the foreign film. The photography is as good as that of the best Holywood pictures. That fact should dissipate the idea that our climate is unsuited to film production. This picture was wholly "taken" in London. And how deliciously is the story of the laughing orange girl handled! Just the right admixture is provided of femininity, merriment, and capriciousness. It is a happy idea, too, on the producer's part to go to Pepys and Evelyn for his sub-titles. One part in the production falls to America. She provides the "star" for the title role in Miss Dorothy Gish. This lady's "Nell Gwyn" is a joyous blend of sparkle, gaiety, and audacity. The other parts are satisfactorily filled, and altogether the film should do much to restore the credit of British-made photoplays.

Glasgow Herald, March 3

THE PLAZA THEATRE.

OPENING PROGRAMME.

A most distinguished and representative audience, which included Prince and Princess Arthur of Connaught and Princess Helena Victoria, was present on Monday as guests of the directors at the private opening of the new Plaza Theatre. The programme, in accordance with the custom followed in the big New York picture houses, comprised several musical selections by the orchestra and organist, and a ballet, " Nell Gwyn," which has aroused so much interest, being relegated to the end. This British film proved, however, well worth waiting for. It is a personal triumph for Miss Dorothy Gish, who gives an interpretation of the pretty and good-hearted orange girl that cannot be praised too highly. There are few moments during the two hours or so the film lasts when Miss Gish is absent from the screen, yet such variety does she impart to her performance and so delightful is her mingled sprightliness and innate innocence that one never wearies of watching her.

Daily Telegraph, March 3

This is the first occasion on which any British film has been bought outright for the world's market before it has been shown to the public. Its exhibition abroad should definitely enhance the prestige of British pictures.

Liverpool Post, December 12, 1925

Dorothy Gish makes a charming hoyden, with just a touch of some faint spiritual beauty in her performance that keeps her Nell always inoffensive —even in her bath scenes.

THE BATH COMPLEX

Baths! What an obsession they are with our American friends! The picture in question received congratulatory notices from the American Press, one of which I feel bound to quote you as the final reply to all the urge and uplift which they offer us If they could only wash their minds in their baths!

Daily Herald, March 6

Randle Ayrton played King Charles II.

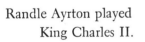

Dorothy Gish

"Daily Express" Cinema Correspondent.

There seems to be a moral in the fact that Miss Dorothy Gish, the famous film star, who is now visiting London, wears her hair unbobbed, while her mother, who is with her, wears it bobbed.

"We have no explanation to offer," said Miss Gish to me yesterday, "except that mothers are getting awfully young."

Miss Gish, asked if she would meet any cinema audiences while in this country, replied :—

"We believe in personal disappearances."

Daily Express, January 10

Brilliant First Night for "Nell Gwyn"

Last night's opening performance at the New Plaza Theatre was a great event in the history of the film. Prince and Princess Arthur of Connaught were present and a host of celebrities in the realms of art, letters, industry, and sport attended. Certainly, no entertainment on so lavish a scale and in so handsome a building has ever been seen in London before in connection with moving-pictures. It is a most striking testimony to the expansion of the film business.

"Nell Gwyn" itself, the most recent of Mr. Herbert Wilcox's pictures, is based on a story by Miss Marjorie Bowen. It is almost wholly a vehicle for Miss Dorothy Gish, who in the title-rôle, gives a meteoric performance, vivacious, roguish, and captivating.

Morning Post, March 2

Courtesy Paramount-British National

LONDON 1927

Thomas Burke's short stories supplied material for many films. Douglas Fairbanks read "The Chink and the Child" and told Mary Pickford it would make a great film. Mary took the idea to D. W. Griffith and that story became "Broken Blossoms." Later Herbert Wilcox used Thomas Burke as the source for Dorothy's picture "London" which was titled "Limehouse" in England.

Courtesy Paramount-British National

John Manners

Adelqui Millar

OPPOSITE. *Photograph by James Abbe*

ANNIE LAURIE   1927

Until this time I was always intimately involved with every aspect of my films. Mother was in England with Dorothy when she had her stroke. We were so deeply concerned for her that I had little to do with "Annie Laurie" and "The Enemy." Both films remain a blur in my mind.

Norman Kerry

All production photographs from the MGM release "ANNIE LAURIE" © 1927 Metro-Goldwyn-Mayer Distributing Corporation. Copyright renewed 1955 by Loew's Incorporated

OPPOSITE. *Photograph by Clarence Sinclair Bull*

Creighton Hale

David Torrence

OPPOSITE. Norman Kerry

Oliver Marsh (Mae's brother) photographing a scene. The director, John S. Robertson, is beside him with Norman Kerry observing.

TIP TOES 1927

Will Rogers adored Dorothy's wit and humor. When they made this film together in London both lived at the Savoy. While they rode to the studio he would try out the jokes he intended using that night in his supper club act on Dorothy. Since he did not need make-up for his part he would bring his typewriter into Dorothy's dressing room, using her as a sounding board while she got ready. He never left her side if he could help it all day long. Then riding back to London in the car he would continue, leaving her flattered but somewhat exhausted twelve hours later.

Nelson Keys and Will Rogers

John Manners

Nelson Keys and Will Rogers

Nelson Keys was a well-known English comedian, so for once Dorothy had more than her share of laughter.

MME. POMPADOUR   1927

Courtesy Paramount-British National

Nelson Keys

The New Photoplays

'Madame Pompadour' at the Paramount— 'Lonesome Ladies' at the Strand.

By JOHN S. COHEN, Jr.

Dorothy Gish is present at the Paramount this week in a made-in-England production called "Madame Pompadour," the subject matter of which is, naturally enough, the favorite of Louis XV. It is a sufficiently entertaining film, not quite up to the standard of "Nell Gwyn," but better than the average British film product. Miss Gish, as usual, is the whole show, in more ways than one, and "Madame Pompadour" as a result will probably be popular in these United States.

Antonio Moreno

THE ENEMY 1928

Ralph Forbes

Metro-*Goldwyn*-Mayer
Presents

LILLIAN GISH
in
"THE ENEMY"
with
RALPH FORBES

Directed by
FRED NIBLO

Based on the Play by
CHANNING POLLOCK

Adapted by
WILLIS GOLDBECK

Continuity by
AGNES CHRISTINE JOHNSTON
and
WILLIS GOLDBECK

Titles by
JOHN COLTON

A METRO-*GOLDWYN*-MAYER PICTURE
Musical Score Arranged by Ernst Luz

Ralph Forbes and director Fred Niblo

Polly Moran

THE CAST

PAULI ARNDT	LILLIAN GISH
CARL BEHREND	Ralph Forbes
BRUCE GORDON	Ralph Emerson
PROFESSOR ARNDT	Frank Currier
AUGUST BEHREND	George Fawcett
MITZI WINKELMANN	Fritzi Ridgeway
FRITZ WINKELMANN	John S. Peters
JAN	Karl Dane
BARUSKA	Polly Moran
KURT	Billy Kent Shaeffer

All production photographs from the MGM release "THE ENEMY" © 1928 Metro-Goldwyn-Mayer Distributing Corporation. Copyright renewed 1956 by Loew's Incorporated

A privileged moment: visiting on the set, the great Russian pianist Ossip Gabrilowitch and his wife, Clara Clemens, the daughter of Mark Twain

George Fawcett,
Frank Currier,
Ralph Forbes,
John S. Peters,
and Fritzi Ridgeway

THE WIND   1928

William Orlamond, Montague Love, and Lars Hanson

The Dorothy Scarborough novel The Wind *seemed written for moving pictures as it depicts constant movement. It blows indoors and out in this small town in Texas. Place a girl reared in the beautiful Virginia countryside in this cyclone and you have conflict. Women, especially, hate sandy winds.*

OPPOSITE. *Photograph by Ruth Harriet Louise*

Dorothy Cummings and Montague Love

Montague Love

Lars Hanson

OPPOSITE. *Photograph by Ruth Harriet Louise*

Our exteriors were shot in the desert around Bakersfield, California. Eight aeroplane propellers created the storm with the help of smoke pots and sand—temperature 120°.

William Orlamond and Lars Hanson

Montague Love

Vladimir Dantchenko, who discovered Chekhov and founded the Moscow Art Theatre, wrote: "I want once more to tell you of my admiration of your genius. A combination of the greatest sincerity, brilliant and unvarying charm place you in the small circle of the first tragediennes of the world.... It is quite possible that I shall write [of it] again to Russia, where you are the object of great interest and admiration by the people."

A dead Montague Love
after shooting him
when he attacked me

As a creative producer, Irving Thalberg was a man of impeccable taste.

DIRECTLY BELOW. Director Victor Seastrom, Johnny Arnold, our head cameraman, Karen (Mrs. Lars) Hanson, and Lars Hanson

BELOW LEFT. Earlier, when Seastrom, Lars, and I were making "The Scarlet Letter," Greta Garbo was also a constant visitor. I believe she felt more secure with her fellow countrymen.

BELOW RIGHT. Dorothy visiting on the set with Victor Seastrom

YOUNG LOVE   1928

Directed by George Cukor

George Cukor: "The extraordinary thing about Dorothy and Lillian—first, of course, their talent—they're very American, their talent is very American, their sticktoitiveness is American—they both have minds—truly American pioneers."

Photograph by James Hargis Connelly

Tom Douglas

Dorothy chose this light comedy for her return to the theatre and found success with it in New York and on the road as well as in London. She was fortunate to have George Cukor as her director. My opening night cable from Europe amused her: "Remember whatever happens your family loves you."

"Young Love" photographs by Bruno—Detroit

Tom Douglas and James Rennie

Late in the twenties I went to Germany to work with Max Reinhardt on a film I hoped to make on the life of Theresa Neumann, the peasant girl of Konnersreuth, famous for her stigmata. Not only had she been without food for two years or water for eighteen months, but in her ecstasy she could speak in any language (normally she could neither read nor write). Hugo von Hofmannsthal was to do our script. During the summer I went to Salzburg and spent several months at Leopoldskron where the three of us worked on the story. Rudolph Kommer, Reinhardt's American manager, became a dear friend as well as our interpreter until I learned a little German. Here with Rudolph Kommer and George Jean Nathan, who stopped by to visit on his trip abroad. Unfortunately, due to the advent of talking pictures, this film was never made.

"Dorothy had all the attributes of a most charming and lovable person and they made her impossible to forget. Her friendship was her greatest gift while her deep family affection guided her whole life."—LAURA MC CULLAUGH

"One would imagine that our two worlds —Lillian's and mine, are worlds apart from each other and could have no common ground on which to build a great and meaningful friendship. There is no way of explaining such things—one can only accept them as a gift."

—NELL DORR

Photographs by Nell Dorr

THIRD DECADE

$\mathcal{T}$HE great depression affected all entertainment. Radio was tops. Bank night was invented to boost the movie box office. Marathon dancing was another proof of desperation, and the elements created the great dust bowl. Those who could afford it kept the legitimate theatre alive. Films turned to big musicals and spectacular dramas while audiences fell in love with a curly-haired moppet named Shirley Temple. Ice skating became the vogue. Noel Coward's "Cavalcade" was heartbreakingly beautiful. Swing was the musical beat. Edward VIII stunned the world by his abdication. The genius of Walt Disney added a new dimension by creating a twelve-reel animated film called "Snow White." Thornton Wilder gave us the classic "Our Town." An enchanting girl took everyone "Over the Rainbow" to meet the Wizard of Oz while war clouds gathered over Europe.

OPPOSITE. *Photograph by Nell Dorr*

WOLVES   1930

Dorothy made her first talking picture for Herbert Wilcox in England in 1930. Because the film was made without a full understanding of the new sound technique, it failed. Dorothy disliked herself so much in it she would never let me see it.

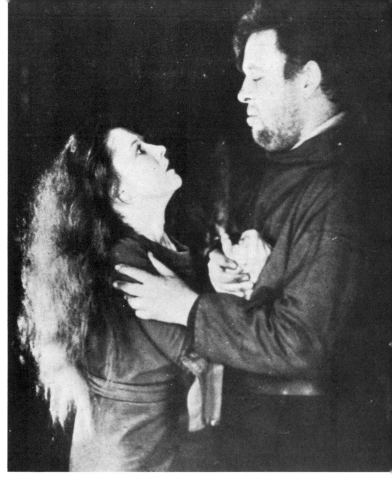

Charles Laughton

"Wolves" was not released in the United States until 1934 and then it was retitled "Wanted Men."

Standing: Charles Laughton, Malcolm Kent (a.k.a. Malcolm Kean), Andrews Englemann, Franklyn Bellamy. Seated with Dorothy is Arthur Margetson.

Courtesy British Dominion

ONE ROMANTIC NIGHT
1930

It seemed so wrong to face a camera knowing that what I was doing could not be understood by most of my friends around the world. I had traveled enough to know how few could speak English and I felt I was betraying a trust (or I felt like a traitor to my followers). Communication in words belonged under the proscenium arch of a theatre, not in a tin box. Following this picture, offers were coming in to make other films, but since I did not sing or dance I made the big decision to go back to where I came from—the theatre—after a seventeen-year absence.

O. P. Heggie and Marie Dressler

Rod LaRocque and Conrad Nagel

"One Romantic Night" was based on "The Swan" by Ferenc Molnar.

Conrad Nagel, Rod LaRocque, Marie Dressler, an unidentified butler, O. P. Heggie, and Billie Bennett

Conrad Nagel

The ball scene

Rod LaRocque

"The Inspector General," From Russia by Way of Jed Harris

THE INSPECTOR GENERAL   1930

We have The New York Times to thank for two of the most endearing men
in the theatre of our century—Al Hirschfeld and Brooks Atkinson.

Photograph courtesy Museum of the City of New York Theatre and Music Collection

UNCLE VANYA   1930

"Uncle Vanya" was the result of a bottle of Clos Vouget wine. While lunching with Ruth Gordon and George Jean Nathan I said it was my favorite of red French wines. She replied that her friend, Jed Harris, had the same opinion. We agreed to a foursome with the first one to find a bottle. It was a thrilling evening for me to listen to Jed's inspired talk about the theatre. When I said goodnight I whispered to Ruth that I would work for him for nothing.

By the end of our first week on the road I had not changed my mind and was surprised to be handed an envelope with, I felt, too much money. To be able to play "Helena" convincingly in a distinguished classic with the best actors in New York was worth more than any salary.

Photograph by L. Arnold Weissberger

Dorothy and I both had the privilege of working with the wonder boy of the theatre, Jed Harris; an association that was never marred by one moment of dissension.

Walter Connolly

Photographs by Vandamm

Isabel Irving, Joanna Roos, Eduardo Cianelli, and Osgood Perkins

One Saturday Isabel Irving's heart stopped as she was on her way to the matinee. Since she had no understudy we found Walter Connolly's wife, Nedda Harrigan, at their home. She rushed over and that dear, brave woman went on, read the part from notes, and kept the curtain up. Nedda later married Joshua Logan.

Osgood Perkins

Joanna Roos

THE STREETS OF NEW YORK
or
POVERTY IS NO CRIME
1931

This amusing satire was an instant hit.

Winifred Johnston

Rollo Peters, Sam Wren, and Romney Brent

Rollo Peters

Fania Marinoff with Dorothy and Armina Marshall at the Westport Country Playhouse, Westport, Connecticut

THE PILLARS OF SOCIETY
1931

Moffat Johnston, Rollo Peters, Armina Marshall, Dorothy, Anton Bundsmann, Leslie Bingham, Romney Brent, and Fania Marinoff

Photograph by Vandamm

Photograph by Irving Chidnoff

THE BRIDE THE SUN SHINES ON
1931

The success of the New York Repertory Company at Westport turned all the cows out of the barns and put the actors in. Since all the plays were not hits, some had to be withdrawn and the idea of repertory was ruined.

Henry Hull

Photographs by White Studio

DAILY NEWS, MONDAY, DECEMBER 28, 1931

"Bride the Sun Shines On"
Is Consistent And Good Fun

By BURNS MANTLE.

SING hey for a Happy Saturday in the theatre! Not one hit, but two, were added to a slightly decimated list of approved entertainments.

"The Bride the Sun Shines On" revealed the most consistently entertaining of current light comedies at the Fulton.

Having a healthy prejudice against that form of comparative criticism that classifies a play as a second this, that or the other; or stamps a play as being definitely better, say, than "Reunion in Vienna," or "Springtime for Henry," I shall not insist that "The Bride the Sun Shines On" is the best light comedy of the year.

But I will say, and without fear of successful contradiction, that it is the most consistent, and certainly one of the most entertaining because of its consistency.

Here, if you are interested, is my notion of believable farce. And when farce is believable it becomes, automatically, light comedy.

Will Cotton's play relates the adventure of Psyche Marbury the day she married Alfred Satterlee, a dull fellow, but sincere.

For years Psyche had been secretly devoted to Hubert Burnet, a young musician.

Hubert, being artistic, was also irascible and difficult. Hubert likewise burned with passion for Psyche, but, fearing she would interfere with what he hoped might be the serenity of his existence, he suppressed his passion.

Now, for her wedding, Hubert has come to play the organ. He is stirred. Psyche is stirred. The family, not knowing why Psyche is as she is, is also stirred. Yet the wedding must and does go on.

"The Bride The Sun Shines On" is a little like Coward's "Private Lives" in the spirit of its fun.

Psyche and Hubert are forever meeting and, out of the intenseness of their love and their tempers, they quarrel and call names. Only to melt next minute into deep regrets and heart sobs. A happy way is found out of their unhappy situation.

"The Bride" should make the New York Repertory Company's season, and I hope it will. Either Lawrence Langner or Knowles Entrikin, who staged it, has employed exceptional sense in casting the play.

Dorothy Gish is the tempestuous bride, believably teetering at the edge of nervous collapse, both amusingly and feelingly in love. Her best performance of any I have seen.

Henry Hull plays the Burnet chap with less uncertainty than he frequently reveals, and few leading men are more effective than he when conditions are right.

Sam Wren is perfect for the disturbed bridegroom, Jessie Busley perfect for the fussy mother, Nicholas Joy a splendid menace and the others, to the least of them, well directed and competent.

I lightly resent, in so consistent a job, the off-key rector of Frank Conlan, but you cannot expect everything of a repertory company. This is too promising an enterprise to discourage with quibbling.

The single setting, the entrance to an organ loft in a private home, is unusual and interesting. Cleon Throckmorton did it.

GEO. M. COHAN THEATRE

SKETCH BY EVERETT SHINN OF **DOROTHY GISH** AS THE BRIDE

THE BRIDE
THE SUN SHINES ON

Photographs courtesy Armina Marshall Langner of The Theatre Guild

CAMILLE   1932

The Central City Opera House in Colorado had been built in the last half of the nineteenth century. It opened with Mojeska playing "Camille." Then Central City was surrounded by gold mines. When they emptied, it became a ghost town. The theatre had been closed for decades when our great designer, Robert Edmond Jones, saw it and realized that the dream of leading Denverites to create an American Salzburg of this picturesque site could become a reality. Bobby restored and added to the grace of an acoustically perfect theatre. He decided to reopen it with "Camille." He would be responsible for everything but the translation of the play and the music, which were done by Mrs. Delos Chappell and Macklin Marrow. Bobby built and painted the scenery, shopped in Hearn's base-

*Photograph by
Ernest A. Bachrach*

Robert Edmond Jones

ment for material remnants, designed my five costumes in different shades of white and those of the other women in the company. With the help of a seamstress, Hilya Nordmark, the entire lot cost less than five hundred dollars. Bobby proved what he believed: that the theatre was a place where it took little money but much talent to create beauty.

Governors from surrounding states came to our opening dressed in the period of the 1880s. Seats were one hundred dollars each but were sold only to those whose ancestors had come West in covered wagons. Afterward the audience went next door to a ball at the Teller House in the same room where General Grant had been feted.

All the great houses of Denver offered their furnishings, even their personal jewels, for our production. A large detective sat in the wings with drawn guns in his hands. He cried so hard during the death scene we didn't dare look his way.

"Camille" photographs by Laura Gilpin

Laura Gilpin is the beloved and trusted photographer of the American Indians.

FOREIGN AFFAIRS   1932

Like Richard Barthelmess in films, we both played opposite Osgood Perkins on the stage.

Henry Hull and Osgood Perkins

Photographs by Vandamm

AUTUMN CROCUS   1932

FRANCIS LEDERER AND DOROTHY GISH

AUTUMN CROCUS

One of the theatre's most distinguished producers, Arthur Hopkins, asked me to be in his first talking picture, "His Double Life," with Roland Young, based on Arnold Bennett's "Buried Alive." He made a delightful film which could have had great success, but studio politics entered and saw to its downfall. A pity, as we needed Hopkins' good taste at that time.

Photograph by Nell Dorr

Roland Young

Courtesy Paramount Pictures

LILLIAN GISH

FROM A PAINTING BY SAVELY SORINI

THE JOYOUS SEASON

BELASCO THEATRE

RIGHT. *Photograph by Pach Studios, courtesy The Walter Hampden Memorial Library at The Players*

NINE PINE STREET   1933

This play was based on the Lizzie Borden murder case.

THE JOYOUS SEASON   1934

The Playbill cover is from a painting by Savely Sorine.

WITHIN THE GATES   1934

Sean O'Casey came to New York for our rehearsals and stayed on for weeks, spending all his time in the audience of the (now) Billy Rose Theatre and in my dressing room between acts. He said, "I can't stay out there. They ask me what my play is about and I don't know what to tell them." When he went home he wrote that he was sorry not to be with us in Philadelphia and when he heard that we were banned in Boston he said he "would have enjoyed hitting out in the center of the fight." I kept his letter, forgive me for quoting. "Let me thank you, Lillian, for a grand and great performance, for your gentle patience throughout rehearsals and for the grand way you dive into the long and strenuous part of the 'Young Whore.'" What a dear, generous man.

Bramwell Fletcher

BY YOUR LEAVE 1934

Very successful actors often go on into other fields. Dorothy's two leading men in "By Your Leave" were Howard Lindsay, the award-winning playwright, and Kenneth MacKenna, Jo Mielziner's brother, who became the story editor for MGM.

Howard Lindsay

BRITTLE HEAVEN   1934

Helen Ray played our Mother in "Her First False Step." Here she is Mrs. Dickinson when Dorothy portrayed her daughter, the poetess, Emily.

Earl McDonald, Helen Ray, and Robert LeSueur standing with Katherine Hirsh and Edward Ryan, Jr.

Photograph by Apeda

Arthur Margetson

Rachael Hartzell

Rachael Hartzell, Leo G. Carroll, and Arthur Margetson

Photographs by
Vandamm

Guthrie McClintic
*Photograph by Editta Sherman,
courtesy Miss Katharine Cornell*

"Hamlet" photographs by Vandamm

Settings and costumes by Jo Mielziner

Sir John Gielgud as Hamlet

As Ophelia   *Photograph by Avery Slack*

Dame Judith Anderson as Queen Gertrude

Judith Anderson, John Emery, and Malcolm Kean

HAMLET   1936

The first time I stepped on a Shakespearean stage was to play Ophelia with the world's finest Hamlet. It was also Judith Anderson's first, as well as the first time Guthrie McClintic had staged Shakespeare. None of us knew how terrified the other was. I looked at "do" and wondered how to pronounce it. Judith told me later she didn't know how to say "good." Then Guthrie asked how we thought he felt directing the man who had staged and played it many times. The Hamlet himself, John Gielgud, acted as if he had never even heard the name and took direction like a child. His behavior during our six-month run won him the adoration of our crew and the entire company. When I complained to Arthur Hopkins that we were closing while playing to standing room after the longest run of any Hamlet, he said, "My dear, don't you know that Hamlet exhausts its Hamlet long before it does its audience."

The ladies on the upper right are Mary Lee Logan, Josh's sister, who was killed so tragically shooting the rapids in 1972, and Evelyn Abbott, who married Keenan Wynn, left the theatre, and later married Van Johnson.

Production photographs by Vandamm

THE STAR WAGON   1937

"After you leave the stage in the first scene as a sixty-five-year-old woman, you enter five minutes later as an eighteen-year-old girl," Guthrie Mc-Clintic told me. Changing the entire costume, removing the white wig, and dressing my hair was easy. For the lightning change of make-up I called on a Russian actress who told me how it had been done in "Chauve Souris." With the help of our dear Reba I was never late during the many months at the Empire or on tour.

Reba started with Dorothy in the twenties and was with her when Mother had her stroke in London. She is still with me and is part of the family.

Reba Hart

Burgess Meredith

On tour we played Detroit in the summer. We stayed out near Grosse Point and rented a speedboat to get us to and from the theatre quickly. It was fun for Burgess, Jane Buchanan, and me.

210

MISSOURI LEGEND 1938

In this play based on the Jesse James legend Dorothy played Mrs. Howard.

Photographs by Vandamm

Dean Jagger

Richard Bishop and Dean Jagger

Jose Ferrer

Margaret Dale, Lucile Watson, and Phyllis Joyce

DEAR OCTOPUS   1939

This play was written by Dodie Smith. Earlier Dorothy had appeared in her play "Autumn Crocus" when she used the nom du théâtre C. L. Anthony. During our run Dorothy was so ill the only thing I remember is that somehow dear Lucile Watson managed to give me the courage to continue working.

"Dear Octopus" photographs by Vandamm

Rose Hobart and Phyllis Joyce

Photograph by Bill Flinn

MORNING'S AT SEVEN   1939

Photographs by Lucas and Monroe

Thomas Chalmers

Kate McComb, Dorothy, Jean Adair, and Effie Shannon

Dorothy was lucky enough to have not one but two talented and charming producers, Guthrie McClintic and Max Gordon.

Herbert Yost, Effie Shannon, Thomas Chalmers, Jean Adair, Dorothy, John Alexander, Enid Markey, Russell Collins, and Kate McComb

LIFE WITH FATHER   1939

The Blackstone Theatre, a mile away from the Rialto in Chicago, had been closed for seven years when this play opened there. It was such an instant success that it revived business in the hotels and shops of the entire district.

    Cecil Smith, the dramatic critic of the Chicago Tribune *said, "Lillian Gish is ideally suited to the part of Vinnie, though a good case could be made in favor of the superior acting technique of her sister, Dorothy, of the Boston-Philadelphia-Detroit company."*

The Pug Scene

Production photographs by Maurice Seymour—New York

Percy Waram as Clarence Day, Sr.

O. Z. "Zebbie" Whitehead as Clarence Day, Jr.

OPPOSITE. *Photograph by Vandamm*

Virgilia Chew as Cousin Cora and
Georgette McKee as Mary Skinner

Jimmy Roland as Whitney and David Jeffries as Harlan

Family portrait:
Jimmy Roland as Whitney, O. Z. White-
head as Clarence, Jr., Peter Jamerson as
John, me as Vinnie, Percy Waram as
Clarence, Sr., and David Jeffries as Harlan

Our First Anniversary party with producer Oscar Serlin, Percy Waram, and Clarence Day's daughter, Peg

It had been my hope to be able to tour "Life with Father" from one end of this beautiful country of ours to another, but after our try-out tour beginning in 1939, we opened February 19, 1940, at the Blackstone Theatre in Chicago and stayed for a record breaking sixty-six weeks, closing May 24, 1941. People came by car and bus from hundreds of miles around to see us which denied me the pleasure of taking this amusing play to them.

BELOW, LEFT. Percy Waram and I indulge in a snowball fight in Grant Park near the theatre where I walked with my West Highland white terrier, Malcolm.

Irene Castle　　Gypsy Rose Lee

FOURTH DECADE

*W*ORLD WAR II raged in Europe. Opposed to the sentiment of 1917 the nation was divided. The America First Organization formed by students at Harvard and Yale quickly spread across the country, but after Pearl Harbor they put on their uniforms and went overseas. Servicemen flocked to the Stage Door and Hollywood canteens. Performers rushed to sell war bonds, join the U.S.O., and entertain the troops. The jitterbug was the dance craze and big band vocalists became stars. "Oklahoma!" revolutionized the American musical theatre and the decade introduced Tennessee Williams. Gasoline was rationed. Laurence Olivier presented a brilliant "Henry V." The film studios, owning their own theatres, unleashed quantity, not quality. Waiting in the wings—television.

LIFE WITH FATHER   1940

When we saw "Life with Father" in New York I was certain this was the play we had been waiting for. Dorothy knew Howard Lindsay, so we went backstage and I asked him if I could have the second company, my sister the third, and Mary Pickford the film rights. He no doubt thought me an odd one since it had just opened. Soon he called and asked if I was serious. But when we went to sign contracts, he and Russel Crouse asked us not to commit ourselves to a long run as they were producing a comedy for the two of us. We asked to see the script. No, it wasn't ready. What's it about? Insanity and murder. A comedy?! We signed run-of-the-play. Their comedy turned out to be "Arsenic and Old Lace."

Walter Kelly as Whitney and
Richard Hudson as Harlan
Photograph by John E. Reed—Hollywood

Other photographs by Vandamm

Louis Calhern as Clarence Day, Sr.

Peter Jamerson as Clarence Day, Jr.

OPPOSITE. *Photograph by Vandamm*

Fay Foto Service of Boston

The Pug Scene

OPPOSITE. This white outfit that Stewart Chaney designed became a classic in the theatre; countless actresses wore it.

Kay Lang as Cousin Cora and Toni Favor as Mary Skinner

Family Portrait: Walter Kelly as Whitney, Richard Noyes as John, Richard Ney as Clarence, Jr., Dorothy as Vinnie, Louis Calhern as Clarence, Sr., and Richard Hudson as Harlan

Photographs by Vandamm

LOVE FOR LOVE   1940

A revival produced by The Players. The Players was founded by Edwin Booth. It is an elegant gentleman's club on Gramercy Park in New York for "players, persons of the press, artists, and men in trade."

Dorothy had the pleasure of being part of this all-star benefit. She was surrounded by friends.

One of Dorothy's favorite vaudeville acts was Clark and McCullaugh. Finally she had the added thrill of working with Bobby Clark and she found him terribly serious, like all great comics.

Edgar Stehli

Photographs by Vandamm

Bobby Clark

"Love for Love" personalities photographed at The Players with His Honor, the Mayor.

TOP ROW: Unidentified, Harold McGee, Thomas Chalmers, Mayor LaGuardia, Comelia Otis Skinner, Dudley Digges, Robert Edmond Jones, Archer Smith, Daisy Belmore. BOTTOM ROW: Barry Jones, Violet Heming, Leo G. Carroll, Bobby Clark, Dorothy, Edgar Stehli and Peggy Wood.

(Photographs courtesy of the Walter Hampden Memorial Library at The Players, New York)

MR. SYCAMORE   1942

This is a whimsical play about a postman (Stuart Erwin) so weary of using his feet that he plants himself in his yard hoping to turn into a tree.

THE PLAYBILL
FOR THE GUILD THEATRE

THE GREAT BIG DOORSTEP   1942

Frances Goodrich and her husband, Albert Hackett, wrote "The Great Big Doorstep." Albert and his brother, Raymond Hackett, both acted with Dorothy in 1922 in a film, "The Country Flapper." Later Raymond played "Armand" to my "Camille."

During one performance Louis Calhern arrived far removed from himself. In spite of cups of black coffee he couldn't remember a line, so Dorothy, as his wife, played both parts, prefacing each line with a "you said" or "you told me" and saved the play for the audience.

Standing: Joy Geffen, Jeanne Perkins Smith, Jack Manning. Seated: Louis Calhern as "Commodore" and Dorothy as "Mrs. Crocket," with Dickie Monahan and Gerald Matthews.

Photograph by Vandamm

Ray Collins and Paul Muni

COMMANDOS STRIKE
AT DAWN 1943

After playing a part for eighteen months without missing one performance you long for two days off. When "Life with Father" closed I needed a change from the theatre. The day director John Farrow told me this film was to be made in Victoria and Vancouver and that he was taking his charming wife, Maureen O'Sullivan, and young son, Michael, with him, I decided this would be my vacation.

Sir Cedric Harwicke, Ferdinand Munier,
Ray Collins, Erville Alderson, and
Rod Cameron

"COMMANDOS STRIKE AT DAWN"
© 1943 Columbia Pictures Industries, Inc.
All rights reserved.

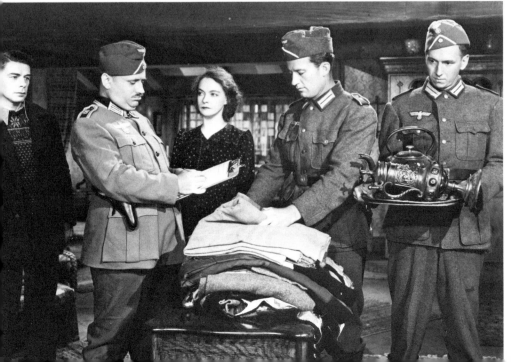

Paul Muni and the Nazis

TOP MAN   1943

Even at this early stage in his career Donald O'Connor impressed me as being extremely talented. Time bore me out.

Richard Dix

Courtesy Universal Pictures

Peggy Ryan, Donald O'Connor, Anne Gwynne, and Richard Dix

Hollywood loved walking scenes: Donald O'Connor, Susanna Foster, and Richard Dix.

OUR HEARTS WERE YOUNG AND GAY   1944

Dorothy insisted this was her talking picture debut, hoping everyone had forgotten "Wolves."

This delightful comedy was based on the reminiscences of Emily Kimbrough and Cornelia Otis Skinner. Three years earlier Dorothy and Cornelia appeared together on Broadway in an all-star version of "Love for Love." Now Dorothy was playing Cornelia's mother.

Members of the cast of "Our Hearts Were Young and Gay": Diana Lynn, James Brown, Bill Edwards, and Gail Russell. Sad that these two lovely girls died so tragically far too young.

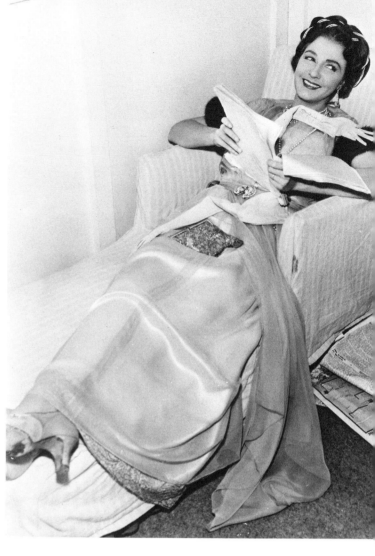

Cornelia loaned me this charming photograph that Charlie Ruggles inscribed to her: "Cornelia—Not Otis but such a proud father of a lovely daughter."

Charles Ruggles and Bill Edwards

Veronica Lake

MISS SUSIE SLAGLE'S
1945

This was a charming story from a novel by Augusta Tucker about a lady who ran a boarding house for struggling medical students. One young intern in a supporting part was Lloyd Bridges who later played the leading role with Dorothy in "The Whistle at Eaton Falls." Oddly enough, Dorothy played my part in the television version for Lux Video Theatre.

Sonny Tufts and Joan Caulfield

Sonny Tufts, Lloyd Bridges, Billy De Wolfe, Pat Phelan, and Renny McEvoy

Courtesy Paramount Pictures

Lillian with Malcolm

Photograph by John Engstead

OPPOSITE. *Photograph by Edward Steichen, courtesy of Mrs. Steichen*

THE MAGNIFICENT YANKEE   1946

"On New Year's Eve, 1945, Mrs. Francis Biddle gave a party for the 'Yankee' company in Washington, D.C. Mrs. Biddle invited many of the (now famous) clerks to Holmes and Brandeis. Her distinguished guest list included Felix Frankfurter, Tommy Corcoran, Dean Acheson, and Ambassador William Bullitt.

At one point during the evening Justice Frankfurter said to Dorothy, 'You were lovely and brilliant but much too pretty for Fanny.'

I entered a strong demurrer at once. In the theatre we always need the extra bit of magic—Dorothy had it. I think Fanny would have approved."—EMMET LAVERY

'Magnificent Yankee' a Beautiful Piece of Sentimental Biography

By JOHN CHAPMAN

I left the Royale Theatre last night in a glow of thankfulness and with a comfortable, warm feeling for the world. I was thankful that Arthur Hopkins, a gentleman of discrimination, had returned as a producing manager. I was thankful that Emmet Lavery had written "The Magnificent Yankee," and that Louis Calhern and Dorothy Gish were playing Mr. Justice and Mrs. Oliver Wendell Holmes. And, in unreasonable conceit—as though it were my very own doing—I was thankful for being an American, and in my pride felt very generous toward everything and everybody.

Not Much Plot.

A play which can stir up this much stuff in any one spectator must be quite a play—and so it is.

Dorothy Gish

A delight, a darling.

But when you sit and look back upon it you discover it isn't much of a play at all, as dramas go. There isn't any plot, because there isn't any conflict. It just dawdles along, telling about a man who was appointed a justice of the Supreme Court of the United States in 1902; a man who was so noble a person that, 31 years later, a new President paid the homage of making a call one scant hour after the President's inauguration.

In this play there is comment on politics, yes; but no politics. Names like Theodore and Franklin Roosevelt, Taft and Wilson figure, and there are characters representing Justic Louis Brandeis, novelist Owen Wister and Henry Adams. Brandeis and Holmes, the two dissenters, talk a bit about important things, like the Schwimmer case. But these names, people and cases are incidents and never dramatically important.

Two Fine People.

The only important thing about "The Magnificent Yankee" is that it is about a magnificent Yankee—and his magnificent wife, and their love one for the other. Mr.

Calhern and Miss Gish have given these characters inspiring decency and great tenderness. Their spoken words of affection are few and mostly bantering, but as they play the roles and as Mr. Lavery has written them the unspoken love story engenders deep emotion.

There is humor, of course; quiet, unforced humor, for Justice Holmes and his wife were Yankees indeed. There is a beautifully conceived and presented sentimental scene in which all of Mr. Holmes' bright young men from Harvard—the secretaries he had year by year—come to congratulate him upon his 80th birthday. There is always a feeling of pride in this country—as when Mr. Holmes bequeathes the bulk of his estate quite simply to the United States of America. And there is heart-wrenching pathos when the justice and his wife face the fact that she is dying and, each in his own way, try to reason it out.

Miss Gish and Mr. Calhern give

"THE MAGNIFICENT YANKEE"
Play by Emmet Lavery, presented by Arthur Hopkins at the Royale Theatre Jan. 22, 1946. Sets by Woodman Thompson. Directed by Mr. Hopkins.

PRINCIPALS:

Mr. Justice Holmes____Louis Calhern
Fanny Dixwell Holmes__Dorothy Gish
Mr. Justice Brandeis___Edgar Barrier
Owen Wister_____Sherling Oliver
Henry Adams_____Fleming Ward

the finest performances I have ever seen them in. She is a delight and a darling. He, besides looking astonishingly like the real Holmes, displays admirable reticence, never once overdoing the Boston accent or the advancing feebleness of an aging man. Together they make the love story of two old people a thing of extraordinary charm.

Mr. Hopkins directed, of course—and with him something the stage has sorely missed has returned. The supporting company is a nice one, and Woodman Thompson's library set gives the proper atmosphere.

Courtesy *New York Daily News*, January 23, 1946

Louis Calhern as Mr. Justice Holmes Dorothy as Fanny Dixwell Holmes

Philip Truex

Louis Calhern, Emmet Lavery the playwright,
and Arthur Hopkins the producer-director

*"The Magnificent Yankee" photographs by
Lucas Pritchard, courtesy of Emmet Lavery*

CENTENNIAL SUMMER   1946

Dorothy was always appalled that she and Constance Bennett were allowed to sing Jerome Kern's beautiful music in "Centennial Summer."

Linda Darnell

Constance Bennet

The family gathers to celebrate their pet's new-born kittens:
Larry Stevens, Linda Darnell, Jeanne Crain, Dorothy,
Walter Brennan, and Barbara Whiting

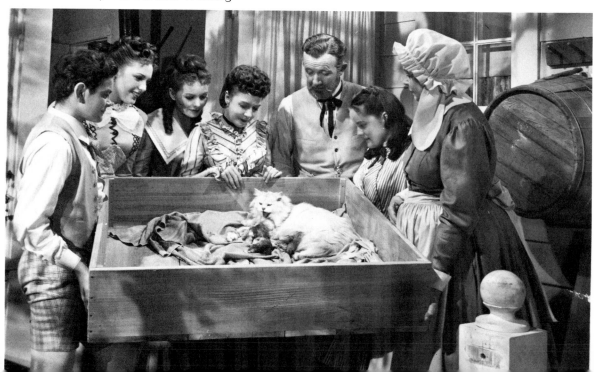

Cornel Wilde, Jeanne Crain, Dorothy, Walter Brennan, Linda Darnell, and William Eythe. In front: Barbara Whiting and Larry Stevens.

Mother and I visit Dorothy on the set along with Walter Brennan, who played her husband, the producer-director Otto Preminger, and our dear Mae Marsh from the Griffith days.

DUEL IN THE SUN   1947

David O. Selznick, a distinguished producer with good taste and endless curiosity about the world, was absorbed with every detail of his pictures, always trying for perfection.

*Lionel Barrymore played my grand-
father at Biograph. Later he played
my father, then my husband. Had he
lived I no doubt would have eventually been cast as his mother. Today
it is not unusual for a man in his
sixties to play opposite a girl in her
twenties.*

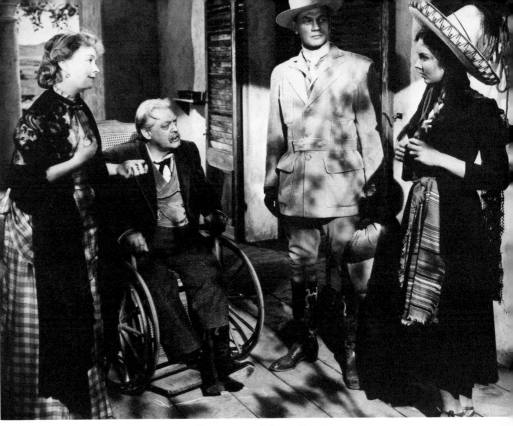

Lionel Barrymore, Joseph Cotten, and Jennifer Jones

Jennifer Jones   Walter Huston

*While we were taking some scenes
with Lionel Barrymore, D. W. Griffith
came to visit us on the set. His presence made Lionel so nervous we had
to stop shooting until Mr. Griffith left.*

CRIME AND PUNISHMENT
1947

In London Rodney Ackland had written the English version of "Crime and Punishment." Anthony Quayle directed it perfectly, resulting in the most popular play of the season. Our distinguished producers Robert Whitehead and Oliver Rea asked Sir John Gielgud to play it here and brought Rodney Ackland over to work with the director, Theodore Komisarjevsky. They quarreled about Rodney's version during the first three weeks of rehearsal, giving us one week's work before the curtain went up in New York. We opened during the great blizzard of '47 to big business and few people, for not a wheel above ground was turning, damaging theatre as well as all other business in Manhattan. Dolly Haas was an adorable Sonia. John, as always, was superb.

Dolly Haas   *Photograph by Fred Fehl*

Sherry Smith and Betty Lou Keim

Sanford Meisner

THE MARQUISE   1947

Mary MacArthur, a lovely child, suddenly found herself to be five feet, six inches tall, but she wanted to still meet her little mama, Helen Hayes, eye to eye, so she was walking with bent knees and stooped shoulders. I thought by taking her away for the summer she would be less self-conscious and stand straight. Richard Aldrich found a Noel Coward play for a seventeen-year-old girl and an older woman which we liked. Arthur Sircom directed it using Eric Coats' music as a background. We had a happy, successful summer.

Photograph courtesy Miss Helen Hayes

Coulter Irwin,
Mary MacArthur
and Cliff Robertson

THE STORY OF
MARY SURRATT 1947

*The story of Mary Surratt was similiar
to Joan of Arc—the miscarriage of justice against two women, Joan for trea-
son against France and Mary for
helping to bring about the assassination of Abraham Lincoln.*

*Dorothy's performnce had such
an emotional impact that I knew I
would have to leave the theatre so as
not to disturb the audience with my
sobbing. When I looked for an easy
exit I found others in the same state.
It proved once and for all that her
gift for tragedy was as great as her
gift for comedy.*

*Dorothy picked the talented Eliz-
abeth Ross to play her daughter. After
Elizabeth married Thomas Noyes,
Dorothy became Godmother to their
first born, Christopher.*

Elizabeth Ross, Dorothy, Richard Sanders and the Union soldiers

*Photographs courtesy The John Patrick Collection,
Boston University*

Elizabeth Ross   *Photograph by John E. Reed*   James Monks

MRS. CARLYLE   1948

This historical play by Glenn Hughes was presented by the University of Washington in Seattle and ran for fifty-one performances, a record for noncommercial theatre.

Joseph Cotten

Courtesy of David O. Selznick Productions

Helen Hayes and I have a moment of fun at the Stork Club.

PORTRAIT OF JENNIE   1949

Locations for "Jennie" were filmed in New York. We spent a lovely week with the unicorns at the Cloisters, which the city allowed us to use for our convent. It was a treat to be associated with David Selznick, Jennifer Jones, and Joe Cotten again.

THE LATE CHRISTOPHER BEAN
1949

"The Late Christopher Bean" was my first television appearance. It was a thrill for us to work in this new medium. Like early movies, it was live—you had only one chance.

Philco Playhouse, N. B. C., February 6, 1949

Helen Carew and Bert Lytell

FIFTH
DECADE

$\mathcal{T}$HERE was a war in Korea called a "conflict." Great live dramas produced by talents like Fred Coe, the unique comedy of Kukla, Fran, and Ollie, and the intelligence of Edward R. Murrow sold television sets by the millions. Legitimate stars transferred their vehicles to this new medium while Hollywood executives chose to ignore it. Simultaneously they were losing their world domination as other countries were making successful films in their own languages. The great romance story was the wedding of beautiful Grace Kelly to Prince Rainier of Monaco. The young filled places like the Peppermint Lounge and brought in Rock 'n Roll. Most important—we had seven years of peace.

OPPOSITE. *Photograph by Guy Gillette*

Composite of Mrs. Savage by Avery Willard —New York

THE CURIOUS SAVAGE
1950

It was my lucky turn to work in a John Patrick play. With Peter Glenville's help I started rehearsals on a Monday and played the Saturday matinee in the lengthy role of the humorous, curious Mrs. Savage.

John Patrick had a working farm in New Jersey. As a witty comment he named two of his prize goats Dorothy and Lillian.

Three of my favorite "Miss Mabel" backstage visitors: Kukla, Ollie, and Burr Tillstrom.
Photograph by Edwin Gray, Falmouth

MISS MABEL   1950

"Miss Mabel" was such a happy success everywhere we went on our summer tour that Joel Schenker wanted to bring it to New York. Fear of its critical reception would not let me risk his losing eighty thousand dollars.

Our dear friends Lawrence Langner and his wife, Armina Marshall, of the Theatre Guild. No one has contributed more to the American theatre.

THE MAN   1950

"The Man" by Mel Dinelli gave Rover, Dorothy's white Pekingese, a chance to play an important role. Ever after when he heard applause he would tear in that direction.

In a short, one-scene part an actor created attention and went on to fame: Richard Boone.

Dorothy with Mel Dinelli. L. Arnold Weissberger took this happy picture of them.

THE WHISTLE AT EATON FALLS
1951

This documentary-type film produced by Louis de Rochemont, in which Dorothy played the widow of the mill owner, was filmed in New England and helped advance the careers of Lloyd Bridges, Anne Francis, Carleton Carpenter, Murray Hamilton, Lenore Lonergan, and Ernest Borgnine.

"THE WHISTLE AT ETON FALLS"
© 1951 RD-DR Corp.
All rights reserved.

Joe Foley, Lloyd Bridges,
and Diana Douglas

Lloyd Bridges and Victor Sutherland

Dorothy with our good friend, Sam LeTulle

BELOW LEFT
On board the R.M.S. "Queen Mary" with my friend
from Triangle-Fine Arts days, Constance Collier

BELOW RIGHT
Seville, April 1952. The Hotel Madrid party at the
end of Semana Santa with Laura McCullough, John and
Elaine Steinbeck, and Charles Bayley

Photograph courtesy Mrs. John Steinbeck

THE TRIP TO BOUNTIFUL   1953

*Fred Coe, in charge of the Philco Hour on early
TV, developed many writers, directors, and actors;
he let his people experiment, stretch their talents,
and see their mistakes. With fifty-two plays a year
it was a great school.*

*When I read the play by Horton Foote I
knew it would take the courage only Fred Coe
would have to produce a story based solely on the
human spirit.*

*When Philco ran it on NBC, the president of
CBS telephoned NBC to say that tonight television came of age. It was the first request of the
Museum of Modern Art for a television film for
their archives.*

*This reaction brought about its opening later
as a play. Eileen Heckart and John Beal did not
play their original roles but Eva Marie Saint repeated her part of one scene so beautifully that
she was picked for the leading feminine role in
"On the Waterfront," which began her long film
career.*

*When the double work hours began to show,
Eva Marie was asked if she wanted her understudy
to play for her. "No," she said, "my loyalty is to
this play. It gave me my break."*

Stage photographs by Eileen Darby of Graphic House

Eva Marie Saint

It was my privilege to introduce our director, Vinnie, to Mary Martin. He directed many of her successes.

Vincent Donehue

Gene Lyons

BROADWAY STARS TOAST LILLIAN GISH

New York; November 19, 1953—Leueen MacGrath, Lucile Watson, Helen Hayes, Janice Rule, Frances Starr, and Betty Field pay an affectionate backstage tribute to Lillian Gish for her magnificent performance in "The Trip to Bountiful," which has been unanimously acclaimed by the critics as the greatest in her career.

THE COBWEB 1955

After reading the first important script on psychiatry, I thought such a story would never have had a chance when I was making films, but I liked and admired all associated with the undertaking so I became a part of it. My instincts seemed prophetic when the reviews claimed that the staff looking after the mentally ill seemed to need more help than their patients.

Confronting Charles Boyer as the old-fashioned doctor

All productions photographs from the MGM release "THE COBWEB" © 1955 Loew's Incorporated

With Lauren Bacall in "The Cat's Paw" scene

Being confronted by Richard Widmark as the revolutionary doctor

Defending Mary Ellen Clemons, Sally Jane Bruce, Gloria Castillo, Cheryl Callaway, and Billy Chapin

NIGHT OF THE HUNTER   1955

Charles Laughton and Paul Gregory turned a bright light on the theatre with "Don Juan in Hell." Then I heard they were spending all their time at the Museum of Modern Art with James Agee, Stanley Cortez, and a staff studying the Griffith films. Soon Charles called me for tea. He told me that they were planning a film on the Davis Grubb novel "Night of the Hunter," for which James Agee was doing the script. He wanted to bring back the unexpected that had been lost since Griffiths best films and asked me to join them. It was a fine story based on good and evil. This was a period in films when "image" was so important that Charles was afraid to make Robert Mitchum play pure evil for fear of ruining his career. Earlier in films an actor would have had a triumph playing evil.

A coffee break for me, a lesson for Sally Jane Bruce from our director, Charles Laughton

Charles Laughton and Paul Gregory

GRANDMA MOSES 1952

It was my good fortune to play the engrossing life of the great American artist. Both of her ancestors came over on the Mayflower.

Schlitz Playhouse, CBS, 1952 March 28
Photograph, IBM, courtesy Galerie St. Etienne

I, MRS. BIBBS 1955

With Richard Kiley, directed by that gifted television director, Richard Dunlap.

Kraft Television Theatre, October 19, 1955

MISS SUSIE SLAGLE'S 1955

Dorothy played my part in the televised version.

Lux Video Theatre, NBC, November 24, 1955

OPPOSITE. *Photograph by Nell Dorr*

THE DAY LINCOLN WAS SHOT 1956

Jim Bishop's best seller cost $600,000 on live T.V., an enormous price at that time. Raymond Massey played Abraham Lincoln, I was Mary Todd and Jack Lemmon portrayed John Wilkes Booth. Charles Laughton narrated.

Ford Star Jubilee, CBS, February 11, 1956

THE CHALK GARDEN
1956

We will always be grateful to Charles Bowden and Richard Barr for our tour of "The Chalk Garden." Later Richard went on to produce the Edward Albee plays and Charles produced several Tennessee Williams plays as well as "The Changing Room" by David Storey.

Posing for publicity stills by Bert and Richard Morgan in Palm Beach, Florida

A performance photo

Three bottom photographs by George E. Joseph

A rehearsal shot

Charron Follett

At the first anniversary party of "Life with Father," for entertainment the producer presented the "accounting scene" from the play performed by a six year old "Father" and six year old Charron Follett playing my part. From that time on the theatre was her obsession. Even now as the equally adorable wife of Richard Traut she divides her spare time away from their three children to act and direct.

This was to be our last curtain call together.

The George Eastman House in Rochester, New York, is a monument to the film industry. They, along with the Museum of Modern Art in New York City and the Library of Congress in Washington, D.C., realize that we are the first century to leave a living record and preserve American film after years of neglect by Hollywood.

It was my privilege to receive two Medal of Honor citations "For Distinguished Contribution to the Art of Motion Pictures" from the George Eastman House.

Mary Pickford and me with our host, the late director of the George Eastman House, General Oscar N. Solbert, in 1955. James Card and George Pratt are two fine young men who carry on his tradition.

Jesse L. Lasky presenting my award, 1955

1957   AWARD WINNERS OF THE SECOND FESTIVAL OF FILM ARTISTS

FRONT, FROM LEFT: Peverell Marley, Harold Lloyd, George Folsey, Gloria Swanson, Lillian Gish, Janet Gaynor, and Mary Pickford.

SECOND ROW, FROM LEFT: Josef von Sternberg, Arthur Edeson, Richard Barthelmess, James Wong Howe, Ramon Novarro, and William Daniels.

BACK ROW, FROM LEFT: Lee Garmes, Frank Borzage, Charles Roshner, and Maurice Chevalier.

Being interviewed for CBS by Mitch Miller, with Janet Gaynor,
Mary Pickford, and Harold Lloyd standing behind us

Photograph by
Robert D. Golding

ORDERS TO KILL   1958

*Anthony Asquith and I had long been
friends before he became one of England's most prominent directors. To
his credit is the film success of George
Bernard Shaw's work.*

*Courtesy Lynx Film released by United
Motion Picture Organization*

Paul Massie

THE FAMILY REUNION   1958

*The first American professional production of this
T. S. Eliot verse play in 1958 with Florence Reed
and Fritz Weaver.*

Phoenix Theatre

PLAYBILL

a weekly magazine for theatregoers

THE FAMILY REUNION

When I read about the Sharon Tate murder case in the New York papers it never occurred to me that the three-hundred-thousand-dollar mansion described was the little cottage Michele Morgan built for twenty-eight thousand dollars on Celia Drive. We rented it one year when Mother, nurse, and Dorothy came west while we were working. No other houses were near so our dogs could run without harm. Here is Dorothy's white Pekingese, Rover, with Mother and me.

With Gracie Fields at her villa in Capri

In Hollywood with Donald Crisp and Mae Marsh

SIXTH DECADE

*A*FTER our period of peace the sixties started with great promise. From the theatre we had the big musicals: "Hello, Dolly!," "Fiddler on the Roof," "Man of La Mancha," and "Hair" as well as Edward Albee's "Who's Afraid of Virginia Woolf?" and John Gielgud's "Ages of Man." From films, the timeless "Sound of Music" and "2001: A Space Odyssey," and from England—The Beatles. With our President's assassination, Jacqueline Kennedy's dignity gave our nation an added dimension. The Viet Nam War tore the country apart. Riots started in our cities and on the campuses. Drugs, pornography, and lawlessness made our streets unsafe. Man reached the moon and a thrill went around the world. Because of film, for the first time we looked from the other side of the moon on into infinity and heard a man's voice saying, "In the beginning was God."

OPPOSITE. *Photograph by Bert and Richard Morgan*

THE UNFORGIVEN 1960

One morning when Audrey Hepburn was thrown from her horse while riding bareback she cracked four vertebrae in her spine. I arrived to find her white and suffering, lying on the ground. They were giving her strong smelling salts to prevent her from lapsing into unconsciousness. She was begging them not to tell the press of the accident until she could telephone Mel Ferrer, then her husband. We were in Durango and she was taken on a stretcher to Los Angeles by plane. In four weeks, long before she should have returned, Audrey came back to work as she didn't want to hold up the company and add to expenses. She was always thinking of others before herself.

Audrey Hepburn

In Durango, Mexico, on location with our director, John Huston

My hair-style I copied from a photograph of my Grandmother Gish.

Charles Bickford and
Audrey Hepburn

THE GRASS HARP   1960

We missed doing "The Grass Harp" and "Arsenic and Old Lace" which were written for two Gishes. I also missed "A Streetcar Named Desire" which was written for one. Later I did do "The Grass Harp" on television for Word Baker and cherish a charming letter Truman Capote wrote me after seeing it. With Georgia Burke and Carmen Mathews.

Jersey Standard, WNTA-TV, March 28, 1960

Photograph courtesy Wagner International Photos Inc.

ALL THE WAY HOME   1960

REAR: Arthur Hill, Aline MacMahon, Edwin Wolfe, Georgia Simmons, Clifton James.
FRONT: John Megna, Colleen Dewhurst, Lenka Peterson and Christopher Month.

Photographed by Irving Penn, © 1961 by The Condé Nast Publications Inc.

Saadoun Al Bayati

A PASSAGE TO INDIA
1963

It is always fun to work with dedicated students in a school like the Goodman Theatre which is part of the Art Museum in Chicago. Saadoun Al Bayati was excellent as Dr. Aziz, making "A Passage to India" a happy success. Pity we don't have the parts to match such talent.

Photograph courtesy New York
Convention and Visitors Bureau

OPPOSITE. *Photograph by
Avery Willard — New York*

This is a pleasant way of "selling the product," judging the 1961 New York
Summer Festival Queen with (standing) Dick Van Dyke of "Bye Bye
Birdie," TV's Richard Hayes, me from "All the Way Home," Gig Young
of "Under the Yum-Yum Tree," James Daly of "Period of Adjustment,"
Henry Fonda of "Critics Choice," Sandra Church of "Under the Yum-Yum
Tree," Richard Cole of Mr. Mort (seated), Mr. Norbert of Elizabeth Arden,
Bettianne Fisch, 1960's New York Summer Festival Queen, and the Fin-
alists: Brenda Cotter, Gretchen Dahm, Eileen Herlihy, Peggy Jacobsen,
Dodie Marshall, and Ann McKeon

TOO TRUE TO BE GOOD
1963

*This group of fine actors banded to-
gether for Shaw's "Too True To Be
Good" for a limited run. The title
fitted our mood perfectly for the opening night party.*

*Two of our three producers were
women, Buff Cobb and Burry Fredrik.
The theatre is one profession where
there is no discrimination between the
sexes.*

Robert Preston, Glynis Johns, David
Wayne, Ray Middleton, Cyril Ritchard,
me, Sir Cedric Hardwicke, Eileen Heckart

THE CARDINAL 1964

This was Dorothy's second film for Otto Preminger and her last motion picture.

Bill Hayes, Tom Tryon,
and Carol Lynley

Maggie McNamara, Carol
Lynley, Tom Tryon,
and Bill Hayes

Maria Tucci as Juliet

Photographs by Friedman-Abeles

ROMEO AND JULIET 1965

There were plans to do "Romeo and Juliet" with Dick Barthelmess in Italy using the original locations, but, following our announcement, letters from the exhibitors begged reconsideration saying Mr. Shakespeare emptied their theatres. By the time I finally succeeded in appearing in this play at the American Shakespeare Festival in Stratford, Connecticut, I was playing the Nurse.

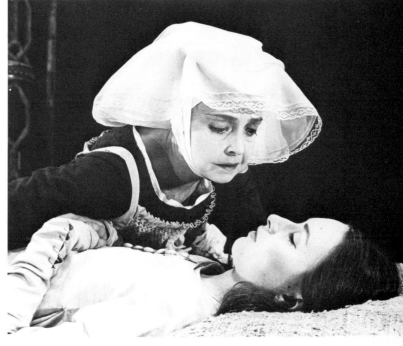

A Juliet offer from Ivor Novello

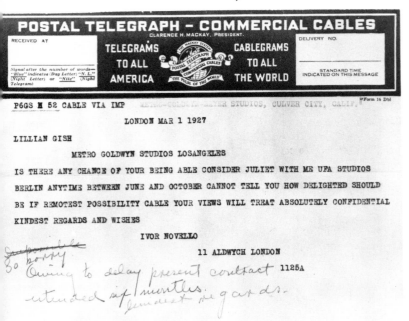

Patrick Hines as Friar Lawrence
and Terence Scammell as Romeo

ANYA   1965

*My first Broadway musical and I loved "Anya."
It is the story of the great legend of our century,
the czar and his family and what happened to
them.*

*We had Rachmaninoff's music and it was so
beautiful. We also had voices from the Metropol-
itan Opera singing the music and we had Constance
Towers who was a lovely "Anya."*

*We played "Anya" previews in New York for
three weeks (the production was much too expensive to tour) and did sell-out business until we
opened and the critics turned thumbs down on us.
I don't know why.*

Opening night with our handsome mayor,
John V. Lindsay, and Constance Towers

A buss from our beloved director,
George Abbott, while Constance Towers
and Irra Petina wait their turn

Michael Kermoyan, our charming
producer, Fred R. Fehlhaber,
Constance Towers, and Irra Petina

Constance Towers   *Photograph by Fred Fehl*
Other photographs by Friedman-Abeles

OPPOSITE. As the Dowager Empress in
a costume by Patricia Zipprodt

FOLLOW ME, BOYS!   1966

Walt Disney's highly imaginative animation has added the most important dimension to film since Griffith.

The Disney energy—Disneyland, Disneyworld, nature films, television, animated cartoons, motion pictures, stage extravaganzas—is overwhelming and unending.

Fred MacMurray   © MCMLXV *Walt Disney Productions*

WARNING SHOT   1967

This was an episodic film. We did not build sets but used actual locations—real apartments with low ceilings so we all were very hot under the lights, but it was a happy experience. Because this was documentary in style I never had scenes with any of the other players.

© *1966 Paramount Pictures Corporation and Bob Banner Associates, Inc.*

I was impressed by the talent of this young actor, David Janssen, and still am. Also, I liked my director and producer, Buzz Kulik and Bob Banner.

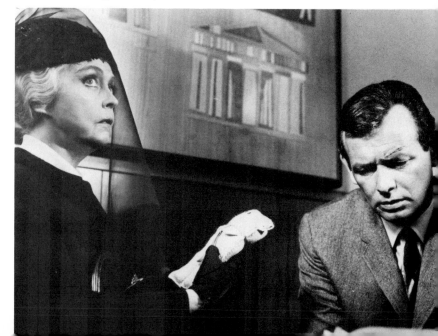

THE COMEDIANS   1967

After working four months in Africa and France with the Burtons, they seemed the opposite of everything I had ever read about them. Elizabeth is a loving, devoted wife and mother. Even the animals preferred her when she came into a room. The day I said goodbye I told her that I might tell the truth about her, destroy her image, and ruin her career.

All production photographs from the MGM release "THE CO-MEDIANS" © 1967 Metro-Goldwyn-Mayer Inc.

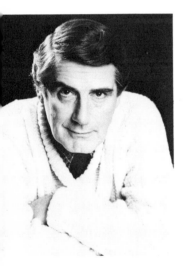

Our gifted director, Peter Glenville. He is so handsome I was sure he was from the aristocracy. I was right. His background is pure theatre.

Photograph by Martha Swope

Paul Ford

Zaeks Mokae and Richard Burton

Elizabeth Taylor

I NEVER SANG FOR MY FATHER 1968

Fine, happy faces reflecting the state of mind of the actors, writer, producer, director—all concerned with "I Never Sang for My Father." Our only heartbreak was to lose Mary Fickett when her part was written out of the play and our concern over the frail health of our talented Alan Webb.

Teresa Wright, Alan Webb, Hal Holbrook, and Mary Fickett

Sloan Shelton, Alan Webb, and Hal Holbrook

Photographs by Martha Swope

ARSENIC AND OLD LACE 1968

My only appearance with Helen Hayes oddly enough turned out to be in "Arsenic and Old Lace."
ABC-TV Production

Next to my Mother the loss of my beloved sister has been my deepest heartache.

In 1928, Mary Pickford, Douglas Fairbanks, Charlie Chaplin and I were asked to visit Russia as guests of their government. Chaplin did not go. My mother was too ill for me to leave her, but Mary and Doug went. Upon their return Mary said, "Don't go. You could not stand so much love." In 1969, I was again invited and went to Leningrad and Moscow for fifteen days to find that they know more about my films than I do. When I gave my illustrated lecture on film the response was overwhelming, as it was everywhere, proving Mary was right. Russia knows the power of film and they use it to show their history, culture as well as the beauty of their country, called "Mother Earth—Mother Russia." This ties their people together. Some great American film-maker should do the same for us.

With Maurice Chevalier when Henri Langlois presented my lecture on the Art of Film at the Palais de Challiot, Paris, 1969

My first cousin, Emily Merrill

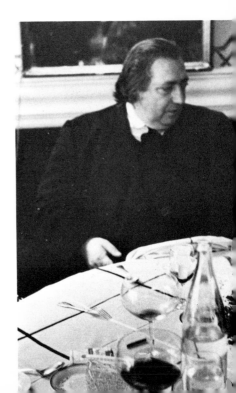

Attending the Sixth International Film Festival at the Kremlin Palace of Congress, July 7, 1969,
In the back row, to my left, are Tamara Gerasimov and my good friend and agent, Lucy Kroll. Also
in this row, fourth from the right, is Marcello Mastroianni and, last, Vittorio De Sica. In the
front row at the extreme right is my host, Serge Gerasimov, the noted director. Over seventy
countries were represented.

We should be proud of the oldest English speaking school in the world teaching drama, the American Academy of Dramatic Art, which is presently at the height of its success due to the continuing work of Worthington Miner and his wife, Frances Fuller.

Henri Langlois and Mary Merson have dedicated their lives to the preservation of the art of film. One of the largest collections of film and memorabilia in the world is housed at the Palais de Chaillot, their monument.

Frances Fuller and Worthington Miner
Photographed at the Waldorf Astoria by Will Weissberg

Henri Langlois dining with me in New York

Colleen Moore and Helen Hayes in Chicago at the beginning of my first transcontinental tour with "Lillian Gish and the Movies." My two dear friends: Colleen since the teens and Helen since the thirties. I am proud godmother of Helen's son, James MacArthur, as well as godmother to his young son, Charles. What a blessing to have life-long friends.
Photograph by Metro News Photos

SEVENTH DECADE

*T*HE war in Viet Nam comes to an end. President Nixon introduces new peace proposals to the world. Youth rediscovers religion. "Jesus Christ Superstar" and "Godspell" reign as Broadway builds new playhouses. Movie cathedrals are gone to be replaced by storefront mini-theatres. Nostalgia brings in "No, No, Nanette." American television gets adult drama from England and Sir Kenneth Clark's *Civilization* sweeps the country. The success of Disneyland gives Florida a Disney-world. Black films come into their own. The pendulum is on the up-ward swing—hopefully.

OPPOSITE. *Photograph by John Engstead*

43rd ACADEMY AWARDS

April 15, 1971
Dorothy Chandler Pavilion
Los Angeles, California

Mr. Melvyn Douglas: *"Here are the faces of Lillian Gish.*

(Melvyn Douglas' delivery of Leonard Spigelgass' introduction broke my heart.)

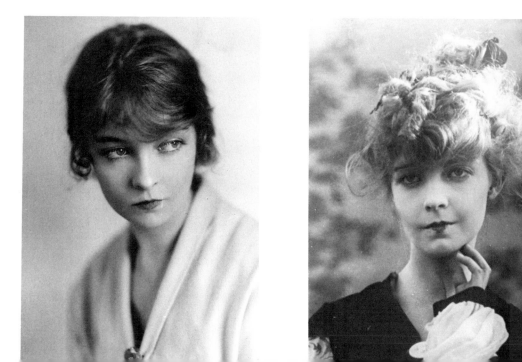

Miss Lillian, as D. W. Griffith used to call her, is the youngest human being in the theatre tonight if youth be measured by zest, enthusiasm, and sheer physical strength. This beautiful woman so frail and pink and so overwhelmingly feminine has endured as a working artist from the birth of the movies to their transfiguration. For underneath this whisp of a creature there is hard steel. In the hundreds of films she has made, she and her beloved sister, Dorothy, coped with danger and peril beyond mortal measure. See for yourselves:

Richard Barthelmess

This is 1920—'Way Down East'—Lillian Gish and Richard Barthelmess on the Connecticut River crossing the ice themselves. No doubles. And privately for you movie buffs, there were twenty-two takes. (There was only ONE take, Melvyn, and we were miraculously alive at the end of it.)

A year later she almost literally lost her head in 'Orphans of the Storm.'

She was highly frustrated at the stocks of 'The Scarlet Letter.'

Thrashed and mauled and beaten by Donald Crisp in 'Broken Blossoms.'

Robert Mitchum

Lars Hanson

And had an unpleasant confrontation with a Hun in 'Hearts of the World.'

And whipped by the wind in 'Wind.'

And she was ready to sacrifice her life in 'Night of the Hunter.'

And put down by a Haitian in 'The Comedians.'

That beleagured girl is a solidly professional actress and I should know because I had the good fortune to direct her some years back in Sean O'Casey's play 'Within the Gates.'

Richard Burton

Charles Boyer

John Gilbert

I found her to be what we call a 'pro' and there's no greater accolade. Oh yes, one. One greater for an actress. To be loved and admired by her leading men. And she ran the gamut—from Richard the Second to Richard the First: Richard Burton, Charles Boyer, Burt Lancaster, Robert Mitchum, Gregory Peck, John Gilbert, Ronald Colman, and Tol'able David himself—Richard Barthelmess.

Richard Barthelmess

Gregory Peck

Miss Lillian has written a book about all this, sternly called, The Movies, Mr. Griffith and Me. Note the order.

In her dedication she wrote:
'To my mother who gave me love
To my sister who taught me to laugh
To my father who gave me insecurity
To D. W. Griffith who taught me it was more fun to work than to play.'

High time we dedicated something to her. And so, to Lillian Gish who has touched all our lives with her gifts, her dignity, her funny little smile, and her immense invulnerability, the members of the Academy and millions and millions of people in the audience say, 'You have taught and keep teaching us that time is an ally, that laughter and tears co-exist, that your starring light is luminous and gentle, yet pierces the darkness.'

Come and get your long overdue Oscar, Miss Gish—Miss Lillian Gish—Miss Lillian—Lillian—"

ACADEMY HONORARY AWARD TO LILLIAN GISH

for Superlative Artistry and for Distinguished Contribution to the Progress of Motion Pictures

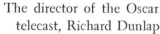

The director of the Oscar telecast, Richard Dunlap

"Oh, I'm speechless. And there are only two words I can say from my beloved sister and myself for this warm tribute from all my friends and all of you of the Academy. Thank you. And for all the charming ghosts I feel around me who should share this. It was our privilege for a little while to serve that beautiful thing—the film—and we never doubted for a moment that it was the most powerful thing—the mind and heartbeat of our technical century. I hope we served it well and I do thank you with all my heart for all of us that this represents. Goodnight."

March 17, 1972

Miss Lillian Gish.

Please excuse me for sending you this note, but I could not get to see you and I am doing this to show my appreciation for what you and your sister did during World War I.

I was walking down one of the streets of Paris with a couple of other soldiers and two young ladies were in front of us and one of the soldiers said that looks like the Gish Sisters. Both of you turned around and said thats who we are, Boys.

I will never forget that. you could have ignored us, but you turned around and talked to us.

You will never know how much we did appreciate your kindness.

Sincerely
John J Hackett
903 Golden Gate Drive
Dayton Ohio 45459

My manager, James Frasher, and Edward Macksoud at Mac-Hugh's in Ridgewood, New Jersey, on an autographing party for *The Movies, Mr. Griffith and Me*

Backstage at the Queen Elizabeth Theatre, April 27, 1973, Vancouver, British Columbia, before a performance under the auspicies of Hugh Pickett for Famous Artists Limited

Photograph by Peter Hulbert for "The Province"

LILLIAN GISH AND THE MOVIES
THE ART OF FILM 1900—1928

Created and produced by Nathan Kroll; films researched and compiled by William K. Everson; edited by Miriam Arsham.

My hope for "The Art of Film" program is to reach the young in colleges, universities and schools who will make our future pictures and to impress upon them the power they leave on the world and to take the responsibility of where they direct this power.

Dignified, Delicate and an Absolute Gas

JOE BALKAKE, *Philadelphia Daily News*, September 29, 1971

Lillian Gish Creates Magic

Her audience, as ever, will need no special markers or Oscar statuettes to signify their feelings about Miss Gish. She will forever be carried in their hearts.

That "star stuff" holds up all right—if the star has the grace and caliber of Lillian Gish.

ROBERT DOWNING, *The Denver Post*, June 28, 1971

"Frankly," explained one rather outspoken student, "I thought she'd turn me right off. She's really something out of the past and all that star stuff just doesn't hold up anymore. But she gassed me. I think I love her."

DON RUBIN, *Toronto Daily Star*, January 9, 1971

UNCLE VANYA   1973

Having been lucky enough to return to the stage from films in the thirties under the unique genius of Jed Harris in "Uncle Vanya," a second blessing came when I was asked to play Marina, the Nurse, under the direction of the brilliant Mike Nichols.

Photographs by Mary Ellen Mark

STANDING: Conrad Bain (Ilya Telyegin), Bernard Hughes (Alexander Serebryakov), George C. Scott (Michael Astrov), Nicol Williamson (Ivan Voinitsky—Vanya), Julie Christie (Elena)

SEATED: Cathleen Nesbitt (Mrs. Voinitsky), Lillian Gish (Marina), and Elizabeth Wilson (Sonya)

Critic at Large

Lillian Gish Shines in 'All the Way Home,' as She and Sister Have in Many Things

By BROOKS ATKINSON

WHEN the curtain goes up on the second act of "All the Way Home" at the Belasco Theatre, Lillian Gish is discovered sitting primly on a sofa, as the deaf and daft mother of a grown family, the audience applauds before she speaks a word.

The audience is applauding one of the pleasantest American legends. For the Gish girls—Lillian and Dorothy—have been through the whole cycle of American show business from road companies in the first decade of the century and the silent films in the second to the theatre of today.

Both of them are about a foot wide and four inches thick, erect and cheerful. Both of them hop around America and Europe whenever anything interests them, and they let out little puffs of enthusiasm as they roll along. They see everything and know everyone. They are as much a part of American folklore as Jack Dempsey, Jimmy Durante and Harry S. Truman. Having been consistently modern for a half century, they give their country continuity.

•

As one of the players in the season's most sensitively acted drama, Lillian is very busy now, changing in and out of wig and costume eight times a week; and, like the other actors, talking on the radio whenever she is bidden, "selling the product," to use her phrase. But if she were not acting a part or crusading for a cause, she would be busy about something else. Probably she would be putting the finishing touches on her book about D. W. Griffith.

She has never been bored in her life. Years ago, when she was billed in the programs on the road as "Baby Alice" or "Baby Ann," she took her first curtain call on the shoulders of Walter Huston in a melodrama called "In Convict's Stripes" or another one called "The Little Red Schoolhouse," she can't remember which. In tow of her mother, May Barnard, an ingenue, she and her sister traipsed up and down the land. They learned how to count by watching the man in the box office, and how to read schoolbooks under their mother's tutelage in dressing rooms and day coaches.

Since her mother had a passion for going through factories, both the Gish girls have a long background in factory culture and to this day they never pass a factory without feeling that they ought to go through it.

When they were in their teens they grew "rather long in the leg," and it was time to make a change. That's how they ventured into the world of the silent film, eventually under the direction of Griffith. Together or individually, they appeared in "The Birth of a Nation," "Intolerance," "Broken Blossoms," "Way Down East" and "The Orphans of the Storm," all of them regarded as film classics today.

Since there was no tradition in film acting, they had to invent one as they went along, and they did. Forty or forty-five years later they are still known and recognized all over the world. When the Moscow Art Theatre undertook to visit America in 1923, Stanislavsky and Nemirovitch-Dantchenko studied the Griffith films in search of a pantomime style that would make Russian actors intelligible in a foreign land, and they found a style they could use.

When Russian actors or dancers come here today they are inclined to study Lillian as if she were a monument. It is a little disconcerting to a gay, incandescent lady who wants to talk and listen.

•

If she radiates general goodwill, it is because she is without vanity. That simplifies her life. She does not have to worry about her dignity or about maintaining a "public image." She is less interested in herself than in in other people, and she is therefore, still learning.

Having had no formal education she has been a reader of all kinds of books since she first discovered the exciting world of culture in the Twenties. Being aware of the world around her, she has little patience with the introspective school of acting. It does not have enough interest in the audience, she thinks. What moves an actor is a matter of no importance, in her view. What moves an audience is.

As one member of a superb company that includes Colleen Dewhurst, Arthur Hill, Aline MacMahon and John Megna, Lillian treats the character she plays in "All the Way Home" as one figure in the delicate fabric of a family play. Everything she does on the stage she does for the play. The applause is for a woman who has always regarded the theatre as an enlightened and practical form of democracy.

—*The New York Times,* Tuesday, December 27, 1960

Brooks Atkinson
Photograph by Campbell, Delmar, New York, courtesy Mr. Atkinson

The loudest and longest ovation at the 1973 Tony Awards was given before it went on the air for Brooks Atkinson, expressing the heartfelt feeling of every one in the theatre world.

Filmography

DOROTHY GISH

1912

AN UNSEEN ENEMY (American Biograph) Director: D. W. Griffith. Scenario by Edward Acker. With Lillian Gish, Robert Harron, Harry Carey, Elmer Booth. Lillian and Dorothy played sisters who are terrorized by a safe-cracker and a drunken maid. Their brother rescues them at the last minute. Although both girls had appeared earlier as extras in audience scenes, this is the first film in which they had featured roles.

THE MUSKETEERS OF PIG ALLEY (American Biograph) A one-reel film directed by D. W. Griffith. With Lillian Gish, Walter Miller, Elmer Booth, Marie Newton, Robert Harron, W. Chrystie Miller, Jack Pickford, Harry Carey. Considered the first important gangster picture, it told of a gang war innocently triggered by Lillian. Dorothy had a small, brief appearance.

GOLD AND GLITTER (American Biograph) Director: D. W. Griffith. Scenario by George Hennessy. With Elmer Booth, Lillian Gish, Lionel Barrymore. A husband goes to a lumber camp where many things happen to him. He gratefully returns to his wife.

THE NEW YORK HAT (American Biograph) Director: D. W. Griffith. Scenario by Anita Loos. With Mary Pickford, Lionel Barrymore, Mae Marsh, Lillian Gish, Robert Harron. Both girls are extras in this Mary Pickford vehicle.

MY HERO (American Biograph) Director: D. W. Griffith. With Robert Harron, Henry B. Walthall, Harry Carey, Charles H. Mailes, Lionel Barrymore, Kate Bruce, Walter Lewis. Misunderstood by their respective parents, Dorothy and Bobby Harron run away. In the wilderness they are saved by an Indian.

A CRY FOR HELP (American Biograph) Director: D. W. Griffith. Scenario by Edward Acker. With Lillian Gish, Harry Carey, Lionel Barrymore, Walter Miller, Claire McDowell, Robert Harron. When a grief-stricken husband attacks a doctor, the doctor's life is saved by a tramp.

OIL AND WATER (American Biograph) Director: D. W. Griffith. Scenario by E. J. Montagne. With Blanche Sweet, Henry B. Walthall, Lionel Barrymore, Charles H. Mailes, Walter Miller, Robert Harron, Alfred Paget, Lillian Gish. Blanche Sweet is the star in this story of a man-of-means who marries a famous dancer. The Gish girls are extras.

1913

THE PERFIDY OF MARY (American Biograph) Director: D. W. Griffith. Scenario by George Hennessy. With Mae Marsh, Lionel Barrymore, Henry B. Walthall, Walter Miller, Harry Hyde. Dorothy and Mae Marsh played cousins who fall in love with the same man.

THE LADY AND THE MOUSE (American Biograph) Directed and scenario by D. W. Griffith. Lillian Gish, Lionel Barrymore, Henry B. Walthall, Robert Harron, Harry Hyde, Kate Toncray. The girls played the daughters of the local grocer, Lionel Barrymore. They befriend a tramp and discover he is a millionaire.

JUST GOLD (American Biograph) Directed and scenario by D. W. Griffith. With Lionel Barrymore, Lillian Gish, Alfred Paget, Charles West, Joseph McDermott, Charles H. Mailes, Kate Bruce. The story of three brothers in search of gold. Lillian played the sweetheart of the fourth brother who stays home to look after their parents. Dorothy's role is brief.

ALMOST A WILD MAN (American Biograph) Director: Dell Henderson. Scenario by William Baudine. With Gus Pixley, Ed Dillon, Charlie Murray. Dorothy falls for an out-of-work actor's performance as a wild man. She discovers he is not so wild after all, but just wild enough for her.

HER MOTHER'S OATH (American Biograph) Directed and scenario by D. W. Griffith. With Robert Harron, Henry B. Walthall, Jennie Lee, Jack Dillon, Charles H. Mailes, Mae Marsh. When Dorothy's mother opposes her marriage, she wishes her blind and elopes with her actor-lover. When an accident does blind her mother the couple return to save her.

PA SAYS (American Biograph) Director: Dell Henderson. Scenario by Anita Loos. With Ed Dillon. When Dorothy's father says her beau is too sissy, her suitor impersonates a woman and the father falls for him/her and is blackmailed into letting Dorothy marry.

THE VENGEANCE OF GALORA (American Biograph) Director: William Christy Cabanne. Scenario by Lionel Barrymore. With Lionel Barrymore, Blanche Sweet, Henry B. Walthall. When a gypsy of the old west, Galora, discovers that the express agent she loves is spoken for by another, she devises an elaborate scheme to involve him in a robbery and her vengeance nearly boomerangs.

THOSE LITTLE FLOWERS (American Biograph) Scenario by Marion Leonard. With Gus Pixley, Gertrude Bambrick, Kate Toncray. Dorothy romps through many misunderstandings over a bouquet.

THE WIDOW'S KIDS (American Biograph) Scenario by Anita Loos. A much-ado-about-nothing comedy with Dorothy playing a comedienne.

THE ADOPTED BROTHER (American Biograph) Directed and scenario by William Christy Cabanne. With Elmer Booth, Robert Harron, W. Chrystie Miller, Charles Gorman. Dorothy is the only daughter of a Western family that has both an adopted brother (Harron) who is virtuous and a blood brother (Booth) who is evil. Dorothy saves Harron when he is attacked by Booth.

THE LADY IN BLACK (American Biograph) Scenario by Anita Loos. With Edward Dillon and Gertrude Bambrick. The hero rescues one maiden from being burned at the stake by Indians and the other, Dorothy, from an unwanted marriage.

THE HOUSE OF DISCORD (Klaw & Erlanger Biograph) Director: James Kirkwood. Scenario by A. Clayton Harris. With Blanche Sweet, Antonio Moreno, Jack Mulhall, Lionel Barrymore, Marshall Neilan. Dorothy almost makes a fatal error in romance but is saved by her mother, Miss Sweet, who years earlier had made the same mistake, thus depriving herself of her daughter's early years.

1914

HER OLD TEACHER (American Biograph) Scenario by Elizabeth Lonergan. With Glen White. Dorothy, in her direst need, is befriended by a spinster teacher. In later years when the teacher is destitute, Dorothy is able to repay her great debt.

JUDITH OF BETHULIA (American Biograph) Director: D. W. Griffith. Based on the apocryphal Book of Judith and the play by Thomas Bailey Aldrich. With Blanche Sweet, Mae Marsh, Henry B. Walthall, Lillian Gish, Robert Harron, Kate Bruce. Mr. Griffith's first feature-length spectacle,

in four reels, starred Blanche Sweet. Later, in 1917, two reels of discarded footage were added, and retitled "Her Condoned Sin" it became Biograph's last release. Lillian played a small part as a young mother and Dorothy had a small role as a crippled beggar.

HER FATHER'S SILENT PARTNER (American Biograph) Director: Donald Crisp. Scenario by Belle Taylor. With Claire McDowell and Harry Carey. Dorothy had a small role in this crook melodrama.

THE MYSTERIOUS SHOT (Mutual-Reliance) Director: Donald Crisp. Adapted from George Patullo's story "The Higher Law." With Donald Crisp, Jack Pickford, Henry B. Walthall. Dorothy, forced by her father to marry a cruel foreman who mistreats her, loves a young Mexican rancher. Several attempts are made on the Mexican's life, but when a mysterious bullet kills her husband, she is free to marry him.

THE FLOOR ABOVE (Mutual-Reliance) Director: James Kirkwood. Based upon E. Phillips Oppenheim's novel *The Mystery of Charlecot Mansions*. With Earle Foxe, Henry B. Walthall, Estelle Coffin, Ralph Lewis. Dorothy as a frivolous but lovable chorus girl helps to unravel the mystery.

THE OLD MAN (Mutual-Reliance) With Henry B. Walthall. Dorothy as a maid-of-all-work finally makes life pleasant for a grouchy old man.

LIBERTY BELLES (Klaw & Erlanger American Biograph) Supervised by D. W. Griffith. With Gertrude Bambrick, Jack Pickford, Marion Sunshine, Reggie Morris, Charles H. Mailes, Spottiswoode Aitken, David Morris, Kate Toncray. A romantic comedy about two boys who get into a girls' dormitory. They masquerade as burglars to save the girls' reputations. Caught and jailed, they are freed when the girls captivate the jailer.

THE MOUNTAIN RAT (Mutual-Reliance) Director: James Kirkwood. Adapted from Mary Rider Mechtold's story. With Donald Crisp, Irene Hunt, Henry B. Walthall. Dorothy plays "Nell, the Mountain Rat," a dance-hall girl whose love regenerates a wastrel.

SILENT SANDY (Mutual-Reliance) Supervised by D. W. Griffith. Scenario by H. R. Durant and Russell E. Smith. With Fred Kelsey. Dorothy plays a romance-starved slavey who places an ad in the matrimonial columns. When a joker answers in the name of a village character known as "Silent Sandy," he marries her rather than humiliate her. Then they truly fall in love.

THE NEWER WOMAN (Majestic-Mutual) Director: Donald Crisp. Scenario by Russell E. Smith. With Donald Crisp and Robert Harron. Dorothy plays an emancipated woman who wants to rule the world. When she is about to lose the man she loves she forgets her new ambitions.

THEIR FIRST ACQUAINTANCE (Majestic-Mutual) Director: Donald Crisp. Scenario by George Hennessy. With Robert Harron, Miriam Cooper, F. A. Turner, W. E. Lawrence, Vester Perry. Dorothy plays a housemaid who naively gets involved in a burglary.

ARMS AND THE GRINGO (Majestic-Mutual) Director: William Christy Cabanne. Scenario by Anna Tupper Wilkes. With Wallace Reid, Fred Kelsey, F. A. Lowery, Howard Gaye. Dorothy as a Mexican señorita in love with Wally Reid becomes involved in contraband as well as romance.

THE SUFFRAGETTE'S BATTLE IN NUTTY-VILLE (Majestic-Mutual) Director: William Christy Cabanne. Dorothy leads the ladies to victory in a battle of the sexes.

THE CITY BEAUTIFUL (Majestic-Mutual) With Wallace Reid. Dorothy falls in love with Reid, fresh from the country, in this Hollywood story. When he fails at a robbery attempt, he gets employed by the studio's prop department.

THE PAINTED LADY (Majestic-Mutual) Supervised by D. W. Griffith. With Blanche Sweet, Josephine Crowell, W. E. Lawrence. Two sisters in the big city. When the younger, Dorothy, falls for a bounder, the elder, Miss Sweet, proves his worthlessness.

HOME SWEET HOME (Mutual) Director: D. W. Griffith. Scenario by Mr. Griffith and H. E. Aitken. Four stories based on the song as reflected in the life of the composer, John Howard Payne. Episode I: Henry B. Walthall, Josephine Crowell, Fay Tincher, Lillian Gish as the sweetheart of the composer, and Dorothy Gish as her sister. Episode II: Mae Marsh, Spottiswood Aitken, Robert Harron, Miriam Cooper. Episode III: Mary Alden, Donald Crisp, James Kirkwood, Jack Pickford, Fred Burns. Episode IV: Courtenay Foote, Blanche Sweet, Owen Moore, Edward Dillon.

THE TAVERN OF TRAGEDY (Majestic-Mutual) Director: Donald Crisp. Scenario by Russell E. Smith. With Donald Crisp and F. A. Turner. Dorothy is a southern tavern keeper's daughter who falls in love with a northerner and saves him from being murdered by her father. They escape together.

HER MOTHER'S NECKLACE (Majestic-Mutual) Director: Donald Crisp. With Howard Gaye and Irene Hunt. Dorothy is jealous of the woman her widowed father wishes to marry.

A LESSON IN MECHANICS (Majestic-Mutual) Director: William Christy Cabanne. With Robert Harron. Dorothy plays a rich girl loved by newly rich Bobby Harron. He is amazed to learn she cares nothing for elegance but prefers to tinker with motors and is mechanically inclined.

GRANNY (Majestic-Mutual) Director: William Christy Cabanne. With Ida Wilkinson, W. E. Lawrence, A. T. Sears. Dorothy and her grandmother, poverty stricken, get jobs washing dishes in a boardinghouse where she falls in love with a new boarder and keeps him from committing a robbery.

A FAIR REBEL (Klaw & Erlanger Biograph) Supervised by D. W. Griffith. With Linda Arvidson, Clara T. Bracey, Charles West, Charles Perley, Walter Lewis, H. Elsky, J. Martin, G. Pierce, Jack Brammall, Robert Drouet, Florence Ashbrook. A romance in three parts with Dorothy playing a Confederate lady in love.

DOWN THE ROAD TO CREDITVILLE (Majestic-Mutual) Director: Donald Crisp. With Wallace Reid. Dorothy as an extravagant young bride-to-be involves her prospective groom, Wally Reid, in such debt that the minister who marries them claims her as his fee.

THE WIFE (Klaw & Erlanger Biograph) Supervised by D. W. Griffith. With Linda Arvidson, Charles West. Dorothy played the ingénue in this film concerning an older woman who marries out of pique. Later she learns that the lover she has flung aside is innocent of her believed wrong.

SANDS OF FATE (Majestic-Mutual) Director: Donald Crisp. With Robert Harron, Cora Drew, Raoul Walsh. Dorothy, Harron, and Walsh are trapped on the desert and put to a grueling test. Dorothy learns which one she really loves.

THE WARNING (Majestic-Mutual) Director: Donald Crisp. Scenario by Russell E. Smith. Dorothy as an innocent country girl dreams she goes to the big city in search of excitement and finds it. Disgraced, she is about to commit suicide when she falls out of the hammock and is awakened.

BACK TO THE KITCHEN (Majestic-Mutual) Director: John O'Brien. Dorothy, as a rancher's daughter, is nearly forced into marriage with a phony Italian count. The cook exposes the fake and enables Dorothy to marry the cowhand she loves.

THE AVAILING PRAYER (Majestic-Mutual) Director: Donald Crisp. Scenario by Richard Barker Shelton. With Spottiswoode Aitken and Raoul Walsh. Dorothy is the ailing daughter of a man who almost makes the mistake of stealing from his employer to pay for sufficient medical aid.

THE SAVING GRACE (Majestic-Mutual) Director: William Christy Cabanne. With George Seigmann and Fred Burns. Dorothy as the illiterate daughter of the town drunkard is educated by a minister. She falls in love with him, but when he spurns her she tries to destroy him.

THE SISTERS (Majestic-Mutual) Directed and written by William Christy Cabanne. With Lillian Gish, W. E. Lawrence, Elmer Clifton. Dorothy gives up the man she loves to Lillian and marries another swain. The sisters are alienated but their respective babies reconcile them and Dorothy makes another sacrifice to ensure her sister's happiness.

THE BETTER WAY (Majestic-Mutual) Directed and written by William Christy Cabanne. Dorothy is a young servant struggling to keep her ex-convict father on the straight path. She succeeds when he attempts to rob the home of her employer.

1915

AN OLD-FASHIONED GIRL (Majestic-Mutual) Director: Donald Crisp. Scenario by Russell E. Smith. With Seena Owen, Eleanor Washington, William Hinckley. This is a pastoral about a pair of country lovers. When the boy becomes infatuated with a city girl only playing with his feelings for the summer, the country girl, played by Dorothy, hides her broken heart.

HOW HAZEL GOT EVEN (Majestic-Mutual) Director: George Seigmann. With Eugene Pallette, Fred Burns, W. E. Lawrence. Dorothy played a restaurant cashier in love with a bus driver whose head is turned when he achieves some success as a prize fighter. She hires a professional boxer to teach her lover and suddenly finds herself attracted to him.

THE LOST LORD LOWELL (Majestic-Mutual) Director: Paul Powell. Scenario by W. Carey Wonderly. With Frank Bennett, Chet Withey, Catherine Henry. Dorothy is an ill-treated maid who falls in love with the next-door butler, a disguised rich nobleman.

MINERVA'S MISSION (Majestic-Mutual) Director: Paul Powell. With W. E. Lawrence, James Gorman, Cora Drew. Dorothy, home from college, starts reforming men from smoking and drinking. When she begins to tell the women how to raise their children, she is thoroughly defeated.

HER GRANDPARENTS (Majestic-Mutual) Director: Frank Powell. With W. E. Lawrence. When Dorothy attempts to desert her elderly grandparents, she relents just in time.

OUT OF BONDAGE (Majestic-Mutual) Scenario by Chester B. Clapp. With William Hinckley, F. A. Turner, Walter Long, Richard Cummings.

An underworld story with Dorothy playing the daughter of a notorious crook. When she is forced to marry his pal, there is a shoot-out with her father and she is free to marry a young orange-grower.

HER MOTHER'S DAUGHTER (Majestic-Mutual) Director: Paul Powell. Scenario by Russell E. Smith. With Mary Alden, W. E. Lawrence, Jennie Lee, F. A. Turner. Dorothy chooses to follow the path of a repentant mother and becomes a nun.

THE MOUNTAIN GIRL (Majestic-Mutual) Director: James Kirkwood. From a Mary Rider Mech-told story. With Frank Bennett, W. E. Lawrence, Ralph Lewis. Dorothy plays a mountain girl who falls in love with a stranger whose life she has saved. When he tries to seduce her, he is killed by her grandfather.

THE LITTLE CATAMOUNT (Majestic-Mutual) Director: Paul Powell. With Ralph Lewis, Frank Bennett, William Brown, W. E. Lawrence. Dorothy is a moonshiner's shrewish daughter fighting off all suitors until a fisherman takes the fight out of her.

VICTORINE (Majestic-Mutual) Director Paul Powell. Adapted from Julian Street's story "The Goings On of Victorine." With Ralph Lewis, Walter Long, Mae Gaston, William Hinckley. Dorothy is a carnival girl who has knives thrown at her by a strong man she worships. When he gets drunk and tries to perform, a young carnie worker who is really the show's angel saves her life and Dorothy soon realizes that she does not worship the strong man.

BRED IN THE BONE (Majestic-Mutual) Director: Paul Powell. Scenario by Russell E. Smith, from a Frank Kinsella story. With Mary Alden, William Hinckley, W. E. Lawrence, Margery Wilson, George A. Beranger, Alberta Lee, Seena Owen, Richard Cummings, Eleanor Washington, Al Filson. Dorothy as a Quaker becomes a famous actress but at the height of her career she renounces it and returns home.

OLD HEIDELBERG (Triangle) Director: John Emerson. Based on the W. Meyer-Forster novel and the Richard Mansfield play. Supervised by D. W. Griffith. With Wallace Reid, Karl Forman, Erich von Stroheim, Madge Hunt, Raymond Wells, Erik von Ritzau, Harold Goodwin, Kate Toncray, Francis Carpenter. Dorothy as the beloved Kathy, a tavern waitress, loves and loses the young Prince Karl, who has been masquerading as a student at Heidelberg.

JORDAN IS A HARD ROAD (Triangle-Fine Arts) Director: Allan Dwan. Screenplay by Mr. Dwan from the Gilbert Parker novel. Produced by D. W. Griffith. With Owen Moore, Sarah Truax, Frank Campeau, Ralph Lewis, Mabel Wiles, Lester Perry, Fred Burns, Jim Ked, Joseph Singleton, Walter Long. Dorothy is protected and aided by her father, a reformed bandit, who never lets her know who he is.

1916

BETTY OF GREYSTONE (Triangle-Fine Arts) Director: Allan Dwan. Scenario by F. W. Pierson. With Owen Moore, Kate Bruce, George Fawcett, Albert Tavernier, Kid McCoy, Warner Richmond, John Beck, Grace Rankin, Eugene Ormond, Marcey Harlan, Leonore Harris. Dorothy, as the daughter of the "Greystone Gables" caretaker, finds romance on the estate but creates a scandal and the villagers force her to leave. When she returns as the wife of the young heir of "Greystone," she is the town's first lady.

LITTLE MEENA'S ROMANCE (Triangle-Fine Arts) Director: Paul Powell. Scenario by F. M. Pierson from his novel Katie Bauer. Produced by D. W. Griffith. With Owen Moore, Marguerite Marsh, Robert Lawler, Fred J. Butler, Alberta Lee, George Pierce, Mazie Radford, Fred A. Turner, James O'Shea, Kate Toncray, William Brown. Dorothy played a Pennsylvania Dutch girl who marries a bona fide count.

SUSAN ROCKS THE BOAT (Triangle-Fine Arts) Director: Paul Powell. Scenario by Bernard McConville. Produced by D. W. Griffith. With Owen Moore, Kate Bruce, Fred A. Turner, Fred J. Butler, Clyde E. Hopkins, Edwin Harley, James O'Shea. Dorothy, as a rich girl with time on her hands, is inspired by her idol, Joan of Arc, to open a slum mission. There she meets the man she weds.

THE LITTLE SCHOOL MA'AM (Triangle-Fine Arts) Directors: Charles M. and Sidney A. Franklin. Scenario by Frank R. Woods and Bernard McConville. With Elmer Clifton, Jack Brammall, George Pierce, Howard Gaye, Luray Huntley, Josephine Crowell, Millard Webb, George E. Stone, Hal Wilson. Dorothy is a Southern girl who goes to teach in a small Western town. She is lonely until she meets a vacationing Virginia playwright. Their romance causes gossip, then scandal, but her devoted pupils set matters straight.

GRETCHEN, THE GREENHORN (Triangle-Fine Arts) Directors: Chester M. and Sidney A. Franklin. Scenario by Bernard McConville from his own story, "Gretchen Blunders In." With Ralph Lewis, Eugene Pallette, Frank Bennett, Kate Bruce, Violet Radcliffe, George E. Stone, Carmen DeRue, Francis Carpenter, Beulah Burns, Tom Spencer. Dorothy as a Dutch immigrant gets involved as a counterfeiter's dupe. When she is kidnapped, a gang of street ragamuffins informs an Italian immigrant who loves and rescues her.

ATTA BOY'S LAST RACE (Triangle-Fine Arts) Director: George Seigmann. Scenario by Tod Browning. With Keith Armour, Carl Stockdale, Adele Clifton, Loyola O'Connor, Joe Nerry, Fred A. Turner, Tom Wilson. Dorothy loves horses but hates racetrack intrigue which had destroyed her father. She nurses "Atta Boy," a lame thoroughbred, and when her husband is desperate for money she enters the horse in a race which is fixed, unbeknownst to her, but "Atta Boy" wins honestly and saves the day.

CHILDREN OF THE FEUD (Triangle-Fine Arts) Director: Joseph Henabery. Scenario by Bernard McConville from his story "The Feud-Breakers." With A. D. Sears, Sam DeGrasse, Fred A. Turner, Elmo Lincoln, Alberta Lee, Charles Gorman, Beulah Burns, Violet Radcliffe, George E. Stone, Tina Rossi, Thelma Burns. This was based on an actual Virginia feud. When the Allens swarm into town and shoot up the courtroom in which one of their clan had been convicted, Dorothy, as the daughter of a moonshiner, wins the town's doctor as her husband.

1917

THE LITTLE YANK (Triangle-Fine Arts) Director: George Seigmann. Scenario by Roy Somerville. With Frank Bennett, Hal Wilson, A. D. Sears, Robert Burns, Kate Toncray, Fred A. Turner, Alberta Lee. Dorothy is a Yankee who falls in love with a Confederate captain who is captured. He is about to be shot when she manages his escape.

STAGE STRUCK (Triangle-Fine Arts) Director: Edward Morrissey. Scenario by Roy Somerville from his story "The Failures." With Frank Bennett, Kate Toncray, Spottiswoode Aitken, Jennie Lee, Mazie Radford, Fred A. Warren. After taking an acting correspondence course, Dorothy comes to the big city to discover the school is a bogus, but succeeds in finding a rich husband.

HER OFFICIAL FATHERS (Triangle-Fine Arts) Directors: Elmer Clifton and Joseph Henabery. Scenario by Roy Somerville from the Hugh S. Miller story "That Colby Girl." With Frank Bennett, Sam DeGrasse, Fred A. Turner, Charles Lee, Milton Schumann, Jennie Lee, Hal Wilson, Fred Warren, Bessie Buskirk. Dorothy is a rich orphan who has control over a bank's board of directors. Two of the directors try to supplant her, one via his handsome son, but she happily marries a lowly clerk.

1918

HEARTS OF THE WORLD (Comstock-World) Subtitled "The Story of a Village. An Old-Fashioned

Play with a New-Fashioned Theme." Produced and directed by D. W. Griffith. Scenario by Mr. Griffith under the pseudonym Gaston de Tolignac. With Lillian Gish, Adolphe Lestina, Josephine Crowell, Robert Harron, Jack Cosgrave, Kate Bruce, Ben Alexander, M. Emmons, F. Marion, Robert Anderson, George Fawcett, George A. Seigmann, Fay Holderness, L. Lowry, Eugene Pouyet, Anna Mae Walthall, Mlle. Yvetter Duvoisin, Herbert Sutch, Alphonse Dufort, Jean Dumercier, Jules Lemontier, Gaston Riviere, George Loyer, George Nichols, Mrs. Gish, Mrs. Harron, Mary, Jessie, and Johnny Harron, Noel Coward. Lillian, a grief-stricken French girl, believes her lover has been killed when the Germans capture her village. Dorothy as the gay-hearted strolling player, "The Little Disturber," literally stole the show. Exteriors and interiors filmed in England; battle scenes behind the lines at Compiègne and St. Liège during World War I.

THE HUN WITHIN (Paramount-Artcraft) Director: Chet Withey. Scenario by D. W. Griffith under the pseudonym Granville Warwick. With Douglas MacLean, George Fawcett, Charles Gerrard, Kate Bruce, Herbert Sutch, Erich von Stroheim, Max Davidson, Robert Anderson, Lillian Clark, Adolphe Lestina. Dorothy has two beaus: one pro-German, the other pro-Allied. She and her Allied beau prevent the other's sabatoge plans.

BATTLING JANE (Paramount-Artcraft) Director: Elmer Clifton. Based on a story by Arnold Bernot. With George Nichols, Katherine MacDonald, May Hall, Ernest Marion, Adolphe Lestina, Bertram Grassby, Kate Toncray. When Dorothy arrives in a small Maine town, she takes care of an orphaned child, forcing a doctor to tend the child's needs.

1919

THE HOPE CHEST (Paramount-Artcraft) Director: Elmer Clifton. Scenario by M. M. Stearns from Mark Lee Luther's novel. With Richard Barthelmess, Sam DeGrasse, George Fawcett, Kate Toncray, Bertram Grassby, Carol Dempster. Dorothy as the daughter of a vaudevillian works in a candy store and falls in love with Barthelmess. His mother tries to break up their marriage but their respective fathers bring about a reconciliation.

BOOTS (Paramount-Artcraft) Director: Elmer Clifton. Scenario by M. M. Stearns from the Martha Pittman story. With Richard Barthelmess, Ed Peil, Fontaine LaRue. Dorothy as a London slavey is in love with an American Secret Service agent who is out to thwart a Communist femme fatale's plot to bomb a peace conference.

PEPPY POLLY (Paramount-Artcraft) Director: Elmer Clifton. Based on a Majorie Raynale story. With Richard Barthelmess, Emily Chichester, Ed Peil. Dorothy is a hoyden in dutch with the law

who falls in love with a young physician, Barthelmess.

I'LL GET HIM YET (Paramount-Artcraft) Director: Elmer Clifton. Based on a story by Harry Carr. With Richard Barthelmess, Ralph Graves, George Fawcett, Porter Strong, Ed Peil. Dorothy as a rich girl goes after a young reporter who thinks he is too busy to be married.

NUGGET NELL (Paramount-Artcraft) Director: Elmer Clifton. Scenario by Hugh R. Osborne, based on John R. Cornish's story. With Raymond Cannon, Regina Sarle, David Butler, James Farley, Wilbur Higeby, Bob Fleming, Emily Chichester. A Western burlesque with Dorothy as a two-gun bandit left with a six-foot-tall baby girl by a miner friend. She ends up happily in the lap of the sheriff.

OUT OF LUCK (Paramount-Artcraft) Director: Elmer Clifton. Scenario by Lois Zellner, from her story "Nobody's Home." With Ralph Graves, Rudolph Valentino, Vera McGinnis, Raymond Cannon, George Fawcett, Norman McNeill, Emily Chichester, Porter Strong, Vivian Montrose, Kate Toncray. Dorothy as a superstitious heroine has fun with astrology and cards but can't decide on a Nordic or a Latin type. A burglar's blackjack settles her problem.

TURNING THE TABLES (Paramount-Artcraft) Director: Elmer Clifton. Scenario by Lois Zellner, from a Wells Hastings story. With Raymond Cannon, Eugenie Besserer, George Fawcett, Kate Toncray, Rhea Haines, Fred Warren, Norman McNeill, Porter Strong. Dorothy is so exasperating to her stern aunt that the aunt has her committed to a sanitarium. Dorothy changes places with a nurse and one of the patients becomes her husband.

1920

MARY ELLEN COMES TO TOWN (Paramount-Artcraft) Director: Elmer Clifton. Scenario by Wells Hastings, from a story by Helen G. Smith. With Ralph Graves, Adolphe Lestina, Kate Bruce, Charles Gerrard, Bert Apling, Raymond Cannon, Rhea Haines. Dorothy is a small-town girl who comes to the city hoping for a stage career. She gets involved as a decoy in a cabaret and her rich suitor takes her home on their honeymoon.

REMODELING HER HUSBAND (Paramount-Artcraft) Director: Lilliam Gish. Scenario by Dorothy Elizabeth Carter. With James Rennie, Downing Clark, Marie Burke, Frank Kingdon. See page 94 for details.

LITTLE MISS REBELLION (Paramount-Artcraft) Director: George Fawcett. Scenario by Wells Hastings, from a story by Harry Carr. With

Ralph Graves, Riley Hatch, George Seigmann, Marie Burke. Dorothy is the grand duchess of a mythical kingdom who escapes a Bolshevik rebellion and comes to the U.S. where she works in a restaurant. She falls in love with an army sergeant who prevents an assassination plot against her.

FLYING PAT (Paramount-Artcraft) Director: F. Richard Jones. Scenario by Harry Carr and F. R. Jones, from a Virginia P. Withey story. With James Rennie, Harold Vizard, Morgan Wallace, William Black, Tom Blake, Kate Bruce, Porter Strong. Dorothy as the wife of an airplane manufacturer is a flying enthusiast. When her husband encourages her to fly the Atlantic he almost loses her to another flyer.

1921

THE GHOST IN THE GARRET (Paramount-Artcraft) Director: F. Richard Jones. Scenario by Fred Chasten (F. Richard Jones), from a Wells Hastings story. With William E. Park, Mrs. David Landau, Downey Clark, Tom Blake, Ray Gray, Porter Strong. Dorothy is banished from the home of her aunt and uncle when they think they've caught her stealing. Hiding out in a "haunted house" she apprehends the real thieves with the help of a secretary whom she loves.

1922

ORPHANS OF THE STORM (See the Filmography of Lillian Gish.)

THE COUNTRY FLAPPER (Producer Security Corp. but part of the Paramount-Artcraft series) Director: F. Richard Jones. Scenario by Harry Carr, from the story "Cynic Effect" by Nalbro Bartley. With Glenn Hunter, Harlan Knight, Mildred Marsh, Tom Douglas, Albert Hackett, Raymond Hackett, Catherine Collins. Dorothy played a "sis Hopkins" character cavorting as if she were a Mack Sennett regular in this story of a bucolic tease.

1923

FURY (Inspiration-First National) Director: Henry King. Scenario by Edmund Goulding. With Richard Barthelmess, Pat Hartigan, Tyrone Power, Sr., Barry Macallum, Jessie Arnold. Dorothy as a Limehouse waif in London waits for Barthelmess who avenges his father by killing the man who ruined his mother.

THE BRIGHT SHAWL (Inspiration-First National) Director: John S. Robertson. Scenario by Edmund Goulding, from the novelette by Joseph Hergesheimer. With Richard Barthelmess, Edward G. Robinson, Mary Astor, Andre de Beranger, Mar-

garet Seddon, Jetta Goudal, William Powell, Luis Alberni, George Humbert, Anders Randolf. Dorothy, as La Clavel, a Cuban dancer, is persuaded by Barthelmess to work with him to get information for the Cuban rebels about the Spanish army. She pays with her life and dies in his arms. Exteriors were filmed in Havana.

1924

ROMOLA (See the Filmography of Lillian Gish.)

1925

NIGHT LIFE OF NEW YORK (Paramount) Director: Allan Dwan. Scenario by Paul Schofield, from the story by Edgar Selwyn. With Rod La-Rocque, Helen Lee Worthing, Ernest Torrence, George Hackathorne, Riley Hatch, Arthur Housman. Dorothy is a telephone operator yearning for the wide-open spaces. A rich man from Iowa with a yen for the big city falls in love with her.

THE BEAUTIFUL CITY (Inspiration-First National) Director: Kenneth Webb. Scenario by Don Bartlet and C. Graham Baker from a story by Edmund Goulding. With Richard Barthelmess, William Powell, Florence Auer, Frank Puglia. The Irish Dorothy loves the Italian Barthelmess. Filmed on New York's Lower East Side.

CLOTHES MAKE THE PIRATE (First National) Director: Maurice Tourneur. Scenario by Marion Fairfax, from the novel by Holman Day. With Leon Errol, Nita Naldi, James Rennie, George Marion, Tully Marshall, Frank Lawler, Edna Murphy, Reginald Barlow, Walter Law. Dorothy is the shrewish wife of Errol. He dreams of being a pirate and gets the chance.

1926

NELL GWYN (Paramount-British National) Director: Herbert Wilcox. Mr. Wilcox's scenario based on the story "Mistress Nell Gwyn" by Marjorie Bowen. With Randle Ayerton, Juliette Compton, Sidney Fairbrother, Edward Sorley, Judd Green, Aubrey Fitzgerald, Hilda Cowley, Dorina Shirley, Gibb McLaughlin, Fred Rains, Johnny Butt, Tom Coventry, Booth Conway, Forrester Harvey, Donald McArdle, Ralph Leslie. Dorothy in the title role in the first English-made film to find a world market.

1927

LONDON (Paramount-British National) Director: Herbert Wilcox. Adapted from a Thomas Burke story. With John Manners, Elissa Landi, Adelqui Millar, Jeff McLaughlin. Dorothy is a Limehouse ragamuffin who is sold into bondage to a Chinaman but manages to escape and find a lover who is an artist. He makes her over into a lady and marries her. Filmed in England where it was retitled "Limehouse."

TIP TOES (Paramount-British National) Director: Herbert Wilcox. His scenario based on a play by Fred Thompson and Guy Bolton. With Will Rogers, Nelson Keys, John Manners. Dorothy as one of three American vaudevillians broke in London poses with her partners as rich socialites to meet English nobility. When a hotel debt forces her to work in a cabaret as a dancer she meets and marries a nobleman.

MME. POMPADOUR (Paramount) Director: Herbert Wilcox. Scenario by Frances Marion, from a play by Rudolph Schanzer and Ernst Wellisch. With Antonio Moreno, Jeff McLaughlin, Henry Bosc, Nelson Keys, Marcel Beauplan, Cyril McLaglen, Tom Reynolds, Marie Ault. Dorothy, in the title role, is Louis XV's mistress, but she falls in love and elopes with Moreno. When they are caught she saves their necks but must part from her lover forever.

1930

WOLVES (British Dominion) Produced and directed by Herbert Wilcox. With Charles Laughton, Jack Ostermann, Malcolm Keen, Arthur Margetson, Griffith Humphreys, Franklyn Bellamy, Andrews Engelmann, Betty Bolton. Dorothy, as a prisoner in a whaling camp, is helped to escape by Laughton who is killed. Herbert Wilcox claims this is the first English all-talkie, even though Alfred Hitchcock's "Blackmail," a far better film, is so credited. "Blackmail" was finished as a silent, remade as a talkie. "Wolves" was planned and shot as a talkie. Released in the U.S. in 1936 as "Wanted Men."

1944

OUR HEARTS WERE YOUNG AND GAY (Paramount) Director: Lewis Allen. Screenplay by Sheridan Gibney, based on the book by Cornelia Otis Skinner and Emily Kimbrough. With Gail Russell, Diana Lynn, Charles Ruggles, Beulah Bondi, Bill Edwards, James Brown, Jean Heather, Alma Kruger, Helen Freeman, Roland Varno, George Renavent, Holmes Herbert, Reginald Sheffield. Dorothy played Cornelia's mother, Mrs. Otis Skinner, in this charming reminiscence of Cornelia and Emily Kimbrough's youth.

1946

CENTENNIAL SUMMER (20th Century Fox)

Produced and directed by Otto Preminger. Screenplay by Michael Kanin, based on the novel by Alfred E. Idell. Music by Jerome Kern. Lyrics by Oscar Hammerstein II, Leo Robin, E. Y. Harburg. Dances staged by Dorothy Fox. In Technicolor. With Jeanne Crain, Cornel Wilde, Linda Darnell, William Eythe, Walter Brennan, Constance Bennett, Barbara Whiting, Larry Stevens, Kathleen Howard, Buddy Swan, Charles Dingle, Avon Long, Gavin Gordon, Eddie Dunn, Lois Austin, Olin Howlin, Harry Strang, Frances Morris, Reginald Sheffield, William Frambes, Paul Everton, James Metcalfe, John Farrell, Billy Wayne, Robert Malcolm, Edna Holland, Ferris Taylor, Winifred Harris, Clancy Cooper. Dorothy played the wife of Walter Brennan, sister of Constance Bennett, and mother of the family.

1951

THE WHISTLE AT EATON FALLS (Columbia) Director: Robert Siodmak. Producer: Louis de Rochemont. Screenplay by Lemist Esler and Virginia Shaler. Story developed from research by J. Sterling Livingston. With Lloyd Bridges, Carleton Carpenter, Murray Hamilton, James Westerfield, Lenore Lonergan, Russell Hardie, Helen Shields, Doro Merande, Ernest Borgnine, Parker Fennelly, Diana Douglas, Anne Francis, Ann Seymour, Joe Foley, Donald McKee, Victor Sutherland, Lawrence Paquin. Dorothy played the widow of the mill owner in this documentary-style film photographed in New England.

1964

THE CARDINAL (Columbia) Producer-Director: Otto Preminger. Screenplay by Robert Dozier. Based on the novel by Henry Morton Robinson. Music by Jerome Moross. Assistant Producer: Martin C. Schute. Costumes by Donald Brooks. Choreography by Buddy Schwab. In Panavision and Technicolor. With Tom Tryon, Carol Lynley, Maggie McNamara, Bill Hayes, Cameron Prud'Homme, Cecil Kellaway, Loring Smith, John Saxon, John Huston, Jose Duval, Peter MacLean, Robert Morse, James Hickman, Berenice Gahm, Billy Reed, Pat Henning, Burgess Meredith, Jill Haworth, Russ Brown, Raf Vallone, Tullio Carminati, Ossie Davis, Don Francesco Mancini, Dino Di Luca, Monks of the Abbey at Casamari, Donald Hayne, Chill Wills, Arthur Hunnicutt, Doro Merande, Patrick O'Neal, Murray Hamilton, Romy Schneider, Peter Weck, Rudolph Forster, Josef Meinrad, Dagmar Schmedes, Eric Frey, Josef Krastel, Mathias Fuchs, Vilma Degischer, Wolfgang Preiss, Jurgen Wilke, Wilma Lipp, The Wiener Jeunesse Choir. Dorothy played the mother of Tom Tryon, the Irishman from Boston who becomes a Cardinal.

Filmography

LILLIAN GISH

1912

AN UNSEEN ENEMY (See the Filmography of Dorothy Gish.)

TWO DAUGHTERS OF EVE (American Biograph) A one-reel film directed by D. W. Griffith. With Henry B. Walthall, Claire McDowell, Elmer Booth. A bit part.

IN THE AISLES OF THE WILD (American Biograph) Director: D. W. Griffith. With Claire McDowell, Harry Carey, Henry B. Walthall. Two trappers fall in love with two sisters, Lillian and Miss McDowell.

THE MUSKETEERS OF PIG ALLEY (See the Filmography of Dorothy Gish.)

MY BABY (American Biograph) Director: D. W. Griffith. With Mary Pickford, Henry B. Walthall, Lionel Barrymore. Small bit part as a bride.

GOLD AND GLITTER (See the Filmography of Dorothy Gish.)

THE NEW YORK HAT (See the Filmography of Dorothy Gish.)

THE BURGLAR'S DILEMMA (American Biograph) Director: D. W. Griffith. With Lionel Barrymore, Henry B. Walthall, Robert Harron. Lionel Barrymore wrote the scenario. He plays the part of a man who tries to blame the murder of his brother on a young burglar, when he actually did it himself.

A CRY FOR HELP (See the Filmograph of Dorothy Gish.)

OIL AND WATER (See the Filmography of Dorothy Gish.)

THE UNWELCOME GUEST (American Biograph) Director: D. W. Griffith. With Mary Pickford, Claire McDowell, Elmer Booth, W. Chrystie Miller, Jack Pickford. Lillian in a bit part only.

1913

A MISUNDERSTOOD BOY (American Biograph) Director: D. W. Griffith. With Robert Har-

ron, Alfred Paget, Lionel Barrymore, Charles Mailes. Lillian, as Bobby Harron's sweetheart, stands by him when he is unjustly accused of murder.

THE LEFT-HANDED MAN (American Biograph) Director: D. W. Griffith. With Charles West and Harry Carey. In this story of a detective clearing an innocent man, Lillian played the love interest.

THE LADY AND THE MOUSE (See the Filmography of Dorothy Gish.)

THE HOUSE OF DARKNESS (American Biograph) Director: D. W. Griffith. With Lionel Barrymore, Claire McDowell, Charles Mailes. Lillian is the wife of a young doctor. Barrymore escapes from an insane asylum and hides in her house. She helps cure him with her piano playing.

JUST GOLD (See the Filmography of Dorothy Gish.)

A TIMELY INTERCEPTION (American Biograph) Director: D. W. Griffith. With Robert Harron, Lionel Barrymore, W. Chrystie Miller, William J. Butler, Joseph McDermott. Lillian is the daughter of an impoverished farmer, Miller, upon whose land oil is discovered. A crooked oil firm is foiled by Bobby Harron.

THE MOTHERING HEART (American Biograph) Director: D. W. Griffith. With Walter Miller, Viola Barry. Lillian is the wife of Miller, who falls for a vamp, but the death of their child reconciles them.

DURING THE ROUND-UP (American Biograph) Director: D. W. Griffith. With Henry B. Walthall, Fred Burns. Lillian is a fickle girl who nearly elopes with a robber, but is saved by her sweetheart.

AN INDIAN'S LOYALTY (American Biograph) Director: D. W. Griffith. With Fred Burns, Eddie Dillon, Dark Cloud. The stunts were more important than the story of this Western melodrama.

A WOMAN IN THE ULTIMATE (American Biograph) Director: D. W. Griffith. With Henry B. Walthall, Charles Mailes. Lillian, the stepdaughter of a scoundrel, refuses to be the decoy in a badger game.

A MODEST HERO (American Biograph) Director: D. W. Griffith. With Walter Miller, Charles Mailes, Harry Carey. While her husband is fishing, Lillian is menaced by a thief.

THE MADONNA OF THE STORM (American Biograph) Director: D. W. Griffith. No further details available.

THE BATTLE OF ELDERBUSH GULCH (American Biograph) Director: D. W. Griffith. With Mae Marsh, Robert Harron, Henry B. Walthall, Kate Bruce, Alfred Paget. During an Indian attack, Lillian is separated from her husband and child. This film is considered an early classic and a forerunner of techniques to come.

1914

JUDITH OF BETHULIA (See the Filmography of Dorothy Gish.)

THE GREEN-EYED DEVIL (Reliance-Majestic) Two reels. With Mary Alden, Henry B. Walthall, Earle Foxe, Ralph Lewis. Details of plot and portrayal not available.

THE BATTLE OF THE SEXES (Reliance-Majestic) Directed and script by D. W. Griffith. Based on "The Single Standard" by Daniel Carson Goodman. With Donald Crisp, Mary Alden, Owen Moore, Robert Harron, Fay Tincher. Lillian pretends to go astray, thus saving her father from deserting the family for a vamp.

LORD CHUMLEY (Klaw and Erlanger) Director: James Kirkwood. Henry B. Walthall, Mary Alden, Charles Mailes, Walter Miller. Lillian is saved from marriage to a crook by a nobleman, Walthall, in the title role. This film dealt with intrigue in upper-class Britain and is from a play long associated with E. H. Sothern.

THE HUNCHBACK (Reliance-Majestic) With Frank Turner, William Garwood, Edna Mae Wilson, T. Haverly. Lillian, as an orphan, is raised by a hunchback peddler. She falls in love with a young prospector. Jealousy is the conflict, until the ending.

THE QUICKSANDS (Reliance-Majestic) With Courteney Foote and Fay Tincher. A two-reel melodrama.

MAN'S ENEMY (Klaw and Erlanger) Three reels. With Franklin Ritchie. Lillian rescues her fiancé from drink and evil.

HOME SWEET HOME (See the Filmography of Dorothy Gish.)

THE REBELLION OF KITTY BELLE (Reliance-Majestic) Director: Christy Cabanne. With Robert Harron, Raoul Walsh. Lillian, a neglected Texas ranch wife, flirts with her neighbor which arouses her husband's jealousy.

THE ANGEL OF CONTENTION (Reliance-Majestic) Director: John G. O'Brien. With Spottiswoode Aitken, George Siegmann, Raoul Walsh. Lillian nurses a wounded cowboy, marries him, and saves him from the gallows.

THE TEAR THAT BURNED (Reliance-Majestic) Director: John G. O'Brien. With John Dillon, W. E. Lowery. Lillian, an innocent country girl, is forced by a city slicker to impersonate a dead girl in order to steal some jewels.

THE FOLLY OF ANNE (Reliance-Majestic) Director: John G. O'Brien. The police want to arrest struggling young author Lillian for vagrancy when she breaks into the home of a publisher.

THE SISTERS (See the Filmography of Dorothy Gish.)

1915

THE BIRTH OF A NATION (Epoch Producing Corporation) Produced under the personal direction of D. W. Griffith. Based on Thomas Dixon's story "The Clansman." Scenario by D. W. Griffith and Frank E. Woods. Music by Joseph Carl Breil. Photography by G. W. Bitzer. With Henry Walthall, Miriam Cooper, Mae Marsh, Josephine Crowell, Spottiswoode Aitken, J. A. Beringer, John French, Jennie Lee, Ralph Lewis, Elmer Clifton, Robert Harron, Wallace Reid, Mary Alden, George Siegmann, Walter Long, Joseph Henabery, Raoul Walsh, Donald Crisp, Howard Gaye, John McGlynn, Ernest Campbell. Lillian played Elsie Stoneman, the daughter of the Northern family, in this Civil War story, the first full-length motion picture.

THE LOST HOUSE (Reliance-Majestic) Director: Christy Cabanne. From a Richard Harding Davis novel. With Wallace Reid, Elmer Clifton, E. A. Turner, A. D. Sears. Lillian, a Kentucky heiress, is rescued by reporter Wally Reid from a burning house where she is being held captive by a scheming uncle and a ruthless doctor.

CAPTAIN MACKLIN (Reliance-Majestic) Director: John G. O'Brien. From a Richard Harding Davis novel. With Jack Conway and Spottiswoode Aitken. Lillian is rescued from the enemy stronghold by her Foreign Legion sweetheart, Conway.

ENOCH ARDEN (Reliance-Majestic) Director: Christy Cabanne. With Wallace Reid, Alfred Paget, D. W. Griffith, Mildred Harris. As Annie Lee, Lillian first marries Enoch Arden, Paget, then his childhood friend Philip Ray, Reid. Mr.

Griffith supervised, produced, and played a minor role as Lillian's father.

THE LILY AND THE ROSE (Triangle-Fine Arts) Director: Paul Powell. Script: Granville Warwick, i.e. D. W. Griffith. With Rozsika Dolly, Wilfred Lucas, Mary Alden, Elmer Clifton, Loyola O'Connor, William Hinckley, Cora Drew. Lillian turns to a former suitor after she loses her husband to a vamp.

1916

DAPHNE AND THE PIRATE (Triangle-Fine Arts) Director: Christy Cabanne. Script: Granville Warwick, i.e. D. W. Griffith. With Elliott Dexter and William Gaye. Lillian is brought from France in 1718 to Louisiana as a "casket bride."

SOLD FOR MARRIAGE (Triangle-Fine Arts) Director: Christy Cabanne. With Frank Bennett, A. D. Sears, Walter Long, Mike Siebert, Olga Grey. Lillian, as a Russian immigrant, is almost forced to marry a brute but escapes to find the right husband.

AN INNOCENT MAGDALENE (Triangle-Fine Arts) Director: Allan Dwan. With Sam DeGrasse, Mary Alden, Spottiswoode Aitken, Jennie Lee. As a Southern belle, Lillian marries an ex-gambler who is falsely jailed but he escapes to return to his wife and child.

INTOLERANCE (Wark) Produced and directed by D. W. Griffith. Photographed by G. W. Bitzer assisted by Karl Brown. Music arranged by Joseph Carl Breil and Griffith. Told in four separate episodes. Lillian rocked a cradle between each part. The Modern Story: Mae Marsh, Fred Turner, Robert Harron, Sam de Grasse, Vera Lewis, Mary Alden, Pearl Elmore, Lucille Brown, Luray Huntley, Mrs. Arthur Mackley, Miriam Cooper, Walter Long, Tom Wilson, Ralph Lewis, Lloyd Ingraham, A. W. McClure, Max Davidson, Monte Blue, Marguerite Marsh, Tod Browning, Edward Dillon, Clyde Hopkins, William Brown, Alberta Lee. The Judean Story: Howard Gaye, Lillian Langdon, Olga Grey, Gunther von Ritzau, Erich Von Stroheim, Bessie Love, George Walsh. The Medieval French Story: Margery Wilson, Eugene Pallette, Spottiswoode Aitken, Ruth Handforth, A. D. Sears, Frank Bennett, Maxfield Stanley, Josephine Crowell, Constance Talmadge (listed on original program as Georgia Pearce), W. E. Lawrence, Joseph Henabery. The Babylonian Story: Constance Talmadge, Elmer Clifton, Alfred Paget, Seena Owen, Carl Stockdale, Tully Marshall, George Siegmann, Elmo Lincoln, George Fawcett, Kate Bruce, Ruth St. Denis, Loyola O'Connor, James Curley, Howard Scott, Alma Rubens, Ruth Darling, Margaret Mooney, Mildred Harris, Pauline Starke, Winifred Westover, and many prominent players played bit and extra parts.

DIANE OF THE FOLLIES (Triangle-Fine Arts) Director: Christy Cabanne. Script: Granville Warwick, i.e. D. W. Griffith. With Sam de Grasse. Lillian as a notorious Broadway dancer is rejected by the society into which she marries.

PATHWAYS OF LIFE (Triangle-Fine Arts) W. E. Lawrence, Olga Grey, Spottiswoode Aitken, Alfred Paget. Lillian loses her husband to a vamp but gets him back this time.

THE CHILDREN PAY (Triangle-Fine Arts) Director: Lloyd Ingraham. Author: Frank E. Woods. With Violet Wilkie, Keith Armour, Ralph Lewis, Alma Rubens, Jennie Lee, Loyola O'Connor. As the older of two children, Lillian refuses to live with either of her divorced parents. The court recommends that she marry her young law student.

1917

THE HOUSE BUILT UPON SAND (Triangle-Fine Arts) Director: Ed Morrisey. With Roy Stuart, Kate Bruce, Josephine Crowell, Jack Brammall, William H. Brown, Bessie Buskirk. Lillian as a pampered debutante rebels against her realistic self-made man but learns to love her husband.

SOULS TRIUMPHANT (Triangle-Fine Arts) Director: John G. O'Brien. With Wilfred Lucas. Lillian's straying husband returns to her.

1918

HEARTS OF THE WORLD (See the Filmography of Dorothy Gish.)

THE GREAT LOVE (Artcraft) Director: D. W. Griffith. Scenario: Capt. Victor Marier (D. W. Griffith and S. E. V. Taylor). With Robert Harron, Henry B. Walthall, Gloria Hope, Maxfield Stanley, George Fawcett, Rosemary Theby, George Siegmann, and as themselves Lady Diana Manners, Miss Elizabeth Asquith, Mrs. Buller, the Duchess of Beaufort, the Princess of Monaco, and Queen Alexandra. A World War I story. Lillian as an Australian minister's daughter marries an American soldier, Bobby Harron, in London. When she inherits a fortune she is pursued by a fortune hunter, Walthall.

LIBERTY BOND SHORT (Artcraft) Director: D. W. Griffith. Kate Bruce, George Fawcett, Carol Dempster. Lillian prefers clothes to Liberty Bonds but changes her mind after a dream where the Huns kill her brother, capture her home, and carry off her mother and sister.

THE GREATEST THING IN LIFE (Paramount Artcraft) Director: D. W. Griffith. Scenario by

Capt. Victor Marier (D. W. Griffith and S. E. V. Taylor). With Robert Harron, Adolphe Lestina, David Butler, Elmo Lincoln, Edward Peil, Kate Bruce, Peaches Jackson. Lillian is a French girl and Bobby Harron an American soldier.

1919

A ROMANCE OF HAPPY VALLEY (Paramount-Artcraft) Director: D. W. Griffith. Scenario: Capt. Victor Marier (D. W. Griffith). With Lydia Yeamans Titus, Robert Harron, Kate Bruce, George Fawcett, George Nicholls, Adolphe Lestina, Bertram Grassby, Porter Strong. Bobby Harron, the boy next door, leaves Lillian behind on the farm when he goes to the big city to seek his fortune.

BROKEN BLOSSOMS (Griffith-United Artists) Directed and written by D. W. Griffith. Based on "The Chink and the Child" by Thomas Burke in *Limehouse Nights*. Photographed by G. W. Bitzer. Special effects by Hendrik Sartov. Technical advisor: Moon Kwan. Music arranged by Louis F. Gottschalk and Mr. Griffith. With Richard Barthelmess, Donald Crisp, Arthur Howard, Edward Peil, George Beranger, Norman Selby (Kid McCoy). Donald Crisp as the father beats his child, Lillian, to death. The Chinaman who loves her, Barthelmess, kills Crisp and commits suicide.

TRUE HEART SUSIE (Paramount-Artcraft) Director: D. W. Griffith. Scenario by Marion Fremont. With Robert Harron, Wilbur Highby, Loyola O'Connor, George Fawcett, Clarine Seymour, Kate Bruce, Carol Dempster, Raymond Cannon. Lillian, as a simple country girl, sacrifices her possessions to help her sweetheart study for the ministry, only to lose him to a milliner.

THE GREATEST QUESTION (Griffith-First National) Director: D. W. Griffith. Story by William Hale. Scenario by S. E. V. Taylor. With Robert Harron, Ralph Graves, Eugenie Besserer, George Fawcett, Tom Wilson, Josephine Crowell, George Nicholls. Lillian is the servant of a brutal farm couple. She knows they are murderers.

1920

REMODELING HER HUSBAND (See the Filmography of Dorothy Gish.)

WAY DOWN EAST (Griffith-United Artists) Produced and directed by D. W. Griffith. Elaborated by Mr. Griffith from the stage play by Lottie Blair Parker. Scenario by Anthony Paul Kelly. With Mrs. David Landau, Josephine Bernard, Mrs. Morgan Belmont, Patricia Fruen, Florence Short, Lowell Sherman, Burr McIntosh, Kate Bruce, Richard Barthelmess, Vivia Ogden, Porter Strong, George Neville, Edgar Nelson, Mary Hay, Creighton Hale,

Emily Fitzroy. Lillian played Anna Moore in this story of a mock-marriage and an illegitimate baby.

1922

ORPHANS OF THE STORM (United Artists) Produced and directed by D. W. Griffith with his adaptation from the Adolphe D'Ennery play "The Two Orphans." With Dorothy Gish, Joseph Schildkraut, Frank Losee, Catherine Emmett, Morgan Wallace, Lucille LaVerne, Sheldon Lewis, Frank Puglia, Creighton Hale, Leslie King, Monte Blue, Sidney Herbert, Leo Kolmer, Adolphe Lestina, Kate Bruce, Fay Marbe, Porter Strong, Louis Wolheim. Lillian brings her blind sister, Dorothy, to Paris in search of an eye surgeon. When they are separated, Dorothy is forced to beg by an old hag and Lillian narrowly escapes the guillotine before they are safely reunited.

1923

THE WHITE SISTER (Inspiration-Metro) Director: Henry King. From the story by F. Marion Crawford. With Ronald Colman, Gail Kane, J. Barney Sherry, Charles Lane, Juliette La Violette, Sig Serena, Alfredo Bertone, Ramon Ibanez, Alfredo Martinelli, Carloni Talli, Giovanni Viccola, Giacomo D'Attino, Michele Gualdi, Guiseppe Pavoni, Francesco Socinus, Sheik Mahomet, James Abbe, Duncan Mansfield. Lillian believes her lover, Ronnie Colman, has been killed, and becomes a nun.

1924

ROMOLA (Inspiration-Metro Goldwyn) Director: Henry King. Scenario by Will M. Ritchey, from the novel by George Eliot. With Dorothy Gish, Ronald Colman, William H. Powell, Charles Lane, Herbert Grimwood, Bonaventura Ibanez, Frank Puglia, Amelia Summerville, Tina Ceccacci Renaldi, Eduilio Mucci, Angelo Scatigna, Alfredo Bertone, Ugo Uccellini, Alfredo Martinelli, Gino Borsi, Pietro Nistri, Alfredo Fossi, Attilio Deodati, Pietro Betti, Ferdinando Chianese, Toto Lo Bue, Carlo Duse, Giuseppe Zocchi, Eugenio Mattioli, Giuseppe Becattini, Rinaldo Rinaldi, Enrico Monti, Baron Winspere, Francesco Ciancamerla, Baron del Judici, Baron Serge Kopfe, Gastone Barnardi, Giovanni Salvini, Countess Tolomei, Marchese Imperiale, Princess Isabella Romanoff, Countess Tamburini, Princess Bianca Raffaello, Marchese Fabrizio Gonzaga, Prince Alexander Talone, Baron Alfredo del Judici, Baron Giuseppe Winspere. Lillian played the title role and Dorothy received top acting honors as Tessa, the Florentine peasant girl tricked into a mock marriage by her seducer, William Powell. She is drowned in the Arno when her lover tries to escape his enemies. Filmed in Florence.

1926

LA BOHÈME (MGM) Directed by King Vidor. Screenplay by Fred de Gresac. Suggested by Henry Murger's "Life in the Latin Quarter." Continuity by Ray Doyle and Harry Behn. Musical scores by Major Edward Bowes and David Mendoza and William Axt. Original compositions by William Axt. With John Gilbert, Renee Adoree, George Hassell, Roy D'Arcy, Edward Everett Horton, Karl Dane, Frank Currier, Matilde Comont, Gino Corrado, Gene Pouyet, David Mir, Catherine Vidor, Valentina Zimina. Lillian was Mimi to Gilbert's Rodolphe.

THE SCARLET LETTER (MGM) Director: Victor Seastrom. Script by Frances Marion, based on the novel by Nathaniel Hawthorne. Musical score arranged by Major Edward Bowes, David Mendoza, and William Axt. With Lars Hanson, Henry B. Walthall, Karl Dane, William H. Tooker, Joyce Coad, Marceline Corday, Fred Herzog, Jules Cowles, Mary Hawkes, James A. Marcus. Lillian plays Hester Prynne in this classic film.

1927

ANNIE LAURIE (MGM) Director: John S. Robertson. Scenario: Josephine Lovett. With Norman Kerry, Creighton Hale, Joseph Striker, Hobart Bosworth, Patricia Avery, Russell Simpson, Brandon Hurst, David Torrence, Frank Currier. Lillian as Annie Laurie in a story of the feuding Scottish clans of the eighteenth century.

1928

THE ENEMY (MGM) Director: Fred Niblo. Scenario by Agnes Christine Johnston and Willis Goldbeck. Based on a play by Channing Pollock. Adapted by Willie Goldbeck. Titles by John Colton. With Ralph Forbes, Ralph Emerson, Frank Currier, George Fawcett, Fritzi Ridgeway, John S. Peters, Karl Dane, Polly Moran, Billy Kent Shaeffer. World War I Vienna with Lillian separated from her husband and facing many miseries.

THE WIND (MGM) Director: Victor Seastrom. Scenario by Frances Marion from the Dorothy Scarborough novel. With Lars Hanson, Montague Love, Dorothy Cummings, Edward Earle, William Orlamonde, Laon Ramon, and others. A Texas prairie windstorm almost drives Lillian insane.

1930

ONE ROMANTIC NIGHT (United Artists) Director: Paul I. Stein. Scenario by Melville Baker, based on "The Swan" by Ferenc Molnar. With Conrad Nagel, Rod LaRocque, Marie Dressler, O. P. Heggie, Billie Bennett, Albert Conti, Edgar Norton, Phillippe De Lacy, Byron Sage, Barbara Leonard. Lillian as Princess Alexandria.

1933

HIS DOUBLE LIFE (Paramount) Directors: Arthur Hopkins and William C. DeMille. Script: Arthur Hopkins and Clara Beranger, based on the novel *Buried Alive* by Arnold Bennett. With Roland Young, Montague Love, Lucy Beaumont, Lumsden Hare. Charles Richman, Oliver Smith, Philip Tonge, Roland Hogue, Audrey Ridgewell. Roland Young as an artist who pretends to be his dead valet happily marries a spinster, Lillian.

1943

THE COMMANDOS STRIKE AT DAWN (Columbia) Director: John Farrow. Script: Irwin Shaw, based on a story by C. S. Forester. With Paul Muni, Anna Lee, Sir Cedric Hardwicke, Robert Coote, Ray Collins, Rod Cameron, Rosemary DeCamp, Alexander Knox, Elisabeth Fraser, Richard Derr, Erville Alderson, Barbara Everest, Louis Jean Heydt, George Macready, Arthur Margetson, Ann Carter, Elsa Janssen, Ferdinand Munier, John Arthur Stockton. Lillian as a Norwegian housewife during the Nazi occupation.

TOP MAN (Universal) Director: Charles Lamont. Script by Zachary Gold, from a story by Ken Goldsmith. With Donald O'Connor, Susanna Foster, Richard Dix, Peggy Ryan, Anne Gwynne, David Holt, Noah Berry, Jr., Marcia Mae Jones, Richard Love, Samuel S. Hinds, Count Basie Orchestra, Borrah Minnevitch's Harmonica Rascals. A wartime musical with Lillian and Richard Dix as parents to Donald O'Connor.

1946

MISS SUSIE SLAGLE'S (Paramount) Director: John Berry. Screenplay by Anne Froelick and Hugo Butler. Additional dialogue by Theodore Strauss. From a novel by Augusta Tucker. With Veronica Lake, Sonny Tufts, Joan Caulfield, Ray Collins, Billy De Wolfe, Bill Edwards, Pat Phelan, Roman Bohnen, Morris Carnovsky, Renny McEvoy, Lloyd Bridges, Michael Sage, Dorothy Newton, E. J. Ballantine, Theodore Newton, J. Lewis Johnson, Ludwig Stossel, Charles Arnt. Lillian, in the title role, ran a boardinghouse for medical interns.

1947

DUEL IN THE SUN (A Selznick International Picture) Produced by David O. Selznick. Directed by King Vidor. Screenplay by David O. Selznick. Adapted by Oliver H. P. Garrett, from the novel by Niven Busch. Music by Dimitri Tiomkin. Costumes by Walter Plunkett. In Technicolor. With Jennifer Jones, Gregory Peck, Joseph Cotten, Lionel Barrymore, Herbert Marshall, Walter Huston, Charles Bickford, Tilly Losch, Joan Tetzel, Harry Carey, Otto Kruger, Scott McKay, Sidney Blackmer, Butterfly McQueen. Lillian is the wife to tyrannical Texas cattle baron Barrymore and the mother of Peck and Cotten, who fight over halfbreed Jennifer. Lionel drives Lillian to drink.

1949

PORTRAIT OF JENNIE (Selznick-United Artists) Produced by David O. Selznick. Directed by William Dieterle. Screenplay by Paul Osborn and Peter Berneis. Adapted by Leonardo Bercovici from the book by Robert Nathan. With a Technicolor sequence. With Jennifer Jones, Joseph Cotten, Ethel Barrymore, Cecil Kellaway, David Wayne, Albert Sharpe, Henry Hull, Florence Bates, Felix Bressart, Clem Bevans, Maude Simmons, Esther Somers, John Farrell, Robert Dudley. Lillian played a nun in this romantic ghost story about a man who falls in love with a girl dead for many years.

1955

THE COBWEB (MGM) Produced by John Houseman. Directed by Vincente Minnelli. Associate Producer Jud Kinberg. Screenplay by John Paxton, based on the novel by William Gibson. In Cinemascope and Eastman color. With Richard Widmark, Lauren Bacall, Charles Boyer, Gloria Grahame, John Kerr, Susan Strasberg, Oscar Levant, Tommy Rettig, Paul Stewart, Jarma Lewis, Adele Jergens, Edgar Stehli, Sandra Descher, Bert Freed, Mabel Albertson, Fay Wray, Oliver Blake, Olive Carey, Eve McVeagh, Jan Arvan, Virginia Christine, Ruth Clifford, Myra Marsh, James Westerfield, Marjorie Bennett, Stuart Holmes. Lillian is on the staff of a posh mental sanitarium.

NIGHT OF THE HUNTER (United Artists) Produced by Paul Gregory. Directed by Charles Laughton. Screenplay by James Agee, based on the novel by Davis Grubb. With Robert Mitchum, Shelly Winters, Evelyn Varden, Peter Graves, Billy Chapin, Sally Jane Bruce, Don Beddoe, James Gleason, Gloria Castillo, Mary Ellen Clemons, Cheryl Gallaway. Lillian is an eccentric but kindly spinster who takes in the children of a maniacal evangelist, Mitchum, after he has murdered their mother.

1958

ORDERS TO KILL (A Lynx Film released by United Motion Picture Organization) Produced by Anthony Havelock-Allan. Directed by Anthony Asquith. Screenplay by Paul Dehn from a story by Donald C. Downes. With Eddie Albert, Paul Massie, James Robertson Justice, Irene Worth, Leslie French, John Crawford, Lionel Jeffries, Sandra Dorne, Nicholas Phipps, Jacques Brunius, Anne Blake. Lillian plays the New England mother of Paul Massie in this Counter-Intelligence story.

1960

THE UNFORGIVEN (United Artists) Produced by James Hill. Directed by John Huston. Screenplay by Ben Maddow from the novel by Alan LeMay. In Technicolor. With Burt Lancaster, Audrey Hepburn, Audie Murphy, John Saxon, Charles Bickford, Albert Salmi, Joseph Wiseman, June Walker, Kipp Hamilton, Arnold Merritt, Carlos Rivas, Doug McClure. Lillian plays the mother of Texas panhandle settlers in the late 1880s.

1966

FOLLOW ME, BOYS! (Buena Vista) Produced by Walt Disney, Co-producer: Winston Hibler. Directed by Norman Tokar. Screenplay by Louis Pelletier, based on the book *God and My Country* by MacKinlay Kantor. In Technicolor. With Fred MacMurray, Vera Miles, Elliott Reid, Kurt Russell, Luana Patten, Ken Murray, Donald May, Sean McClory, Steve Franken, Parley Baer, William Reynolds, Lem's Boys, Craig Hill, Tol Avery, John Zaremba, Willis Bouchey, Madge Blake, Carl Reindel, Hank Brandt, Richard Bakalyan, Tim McIntire, Willie Soo Hoo, Tony Regan, Robert B. Williams, Jimmy Murphy, Adam Williams. Lillian played "Hetty Seibert" in this Boy Scouts' story.

1967

WARNING SHOT (Paramount) Produced by Bob Banner. Directed by Buzz Kulik. Screenplay by Mann Rubin. In Technicolor. With David Janssen, Ed Begley, Keenan Wynn, Sam Wanamaker, Eleanor Parker, Stefanie Powers, George Grizzard, George Sanders, Steve Allen, Carroll O'Connor, Joan Collins, Donald Curtis, Walter Pidgeon, John Garfield, Jr. Lillian played "Alice Willows" in this episodic murder mystery.

THE COMEDIANS (MGM) Produced and directed by Peter Glenville. Screenplay by Graham Green from his novel. In Technicolor. With Elizabeth Taylor, Richard Burton, Alec Guinness, Peter Ustinov, Paul Ford, Raymond St. Jacques, Zaeks Mokae, Roscoe Lee Browne, Douta Seck, Aliba Peters, Gloria Foster, Robin Langford, Georg Stanford Brown, James Earl Jones, Cicely Tyson. Lillian plays the silly American wife of the equally silly Paul Ford, who had run for President on the vegetarian ticket.

Stageography

DOROTHY GISH

1928

YOUNG LOVE. A comedy in three acts by Samson Raphaelson. Produced by Kenneth MacGowan and Sidney Ross at the Masque Theatre, October 30, 1928. Staged by George Cukor. With Tom Douglas, James Rennie, Catherine Willard. Played Hilary.

1929

YOUNG LOVE. Re-created the role of Hilary in London at the Arts Theatre, July 3, 1929. Produced by George Zucco. With Frank Conroy, Fabia Drake, Derrick de Marney.

1930

THE INSPECTOR GENERAL. A farce comedy in three acts adapted by John Anderson from the Russian of Nicolai Gogol. Revived, produced, and staged by Jed Harris at the Hudson Theatre, December 23, 1930. With Josef Lozarvici, Frank Conlan, Theodore Hart, Claude Cooper, Eugene Powers, Eduardo Ciannelli, Edward Rigby, Owen Meech, Joseph Sauers, Con MacSunday, Lina Arbarbanell, J. Edward Bromberg, William Challee, Romney Brent, Bessie Traub, William Dorbin, Harold Johnsrud, Flavia Arcaro. Played Marya.

1931

GETTING MARRIED. A comedy without intermission by George Bernard Shaw. Revived by the Theatre Guild at the Guild Theatre, March 30, 1931. Staged by Philip Moeller. With Margaret Wycherly, Henry Travers, Ernest Cossart, Irby Marshall, Hugh Buckler, Reginald Mason, Hugh Sinclair, Romney Brent, Peg Entwistle, Ralph Roeder, Helen Westley, Oscar Serling. Played Leo.

1931

THE STREETS OF NEW YORK, OR POVERTY IS NO CRIME. A melodrama in five acts by Dion Boucicault. Revived by the New York Repertory Company at the Forty-eighth Street Theatre, October 6, 1931. Staged by Knowles Entrikin. With Rollo Peters, Romney Brent, Moffat Johnston, Fania Marinoff, Jessie Busley, Frank Conlan, Sam Wren, A. P. Kaye, Winifred Johnston, Mervin Williams, Jock Munro, Anton Bundsmann, Robert Turney, Eleanor Shaler, Russell Rhodes, Alvin Barrett, Ronald Jones, Barbara Childs, Ann Tewksbury, Cecilia Lenihan, Nancy McKnight. Played Lucy Fairweather.

1931

THE PILLARS OF SOCIETY. A drama in three acts by Henrik Ibsen. Revived by the New York Repertory Company at the Forty-eighth Street Theatre, October 14, 1931. Staged by Winifred Lenihan. With Moffat Johnston, Ann Dere, Richard Jack, Fania Marinoff, Rollo Peters, Armina Marshall, Romney Brent, Knowles Entrikin, Edgar Stehli, Frank Conlan, Jessie Busley, Eleanor Shaler, Ann Tewksbury, Barbara Child, Cecilia Lenihan, Robert Lowe, Dudley Hawley, Sam Wren, Russell Rhodes, Anton Bundsmann, Alvin Barrett, Robert Turney, Mervin Williams, Ronald Jones, Jock Munro, Virginia Volland, Nancy McKnight. Played Dina Dorf.

1931

THE BRIDE THE SUN SHINES ON. A comedy in three acts by Will Cotton. Produced by the New York Repertory Company at the Fulton Theatre, December 26, 1931. Staged by Knowles Entrikin. With Jessie Busley, Russell Rhodes, Dudley Hawley, Fania Marinoff, Henry Hull, Sam Wren, Nicholas Joy, Armina Marshall, Frank Conlon, Eleanor Shaler, Mervin Williams, Ann Tewksbury, Anita Heller, Barbara Child, Helen Dedens, Janet Langhorne, Muriel Chase, Alvin Barrett, Anton Bundsmann, Ronald Jones, Jock Munro, Robert Turney. Played Psyche Marbury.

1932

FOREIGN AFFAIRS. A romantic comedy in three acts by Paul Hervey Fox and George Tilton. Produced by B. Franklin Kamsler and Lester Fuller at the Avon Theatre, April 13, 1932. Staged by Lester Fuller. With Henry Hull, Edouard La Roche, Osgood Perkins, Jean Arthur, J. Edward Bromberg, Carl Benton Reid. Played the Countess Isla Da Cassali.

1932

AUTUMN CROCUS. A play in three acts by C. L. Anthony. Produced by Lee Shubert in association with Basil Dean and directed by Mr. Dean at the Morosco Theatre, November 19, 1932. With Francis Lederer, Evamarie Hechtl, Minna Phillips, Eda Heinemann, Marcella Swanson, Lowell Gilmore, Charles H. Croker-King, Margaret Arrow, Robert C. Fischer, Dagmar Hampf, Hella Henrichs. Played The Lady in Spectacles.

1934

BY YOUR LEAVE. A comedy in three acts by Gladys Hurlbut and Emma Wells. Produced by Richard Aldrich and Alfred de Liagre, Jr. at the Morosco Theatre, January 24, 1934. Staged by Alfred de Liagre, Jr. Settings by Jo Mielziner. With Josephine Hull, Esther Dale, Elizabeth Bruce, Howard Lindsay, Cynthia Rogers, Kenneth MacKenna, Ernest Glendinning, Elizabeth Love, Henry Fox, Thomas Hayes. Played Ellen Smith.

1934

BRITTLE HEAVEN. A drama in three acts adapted by Vincent York and Frederick Pohl from Josephine Pollitt's book "Emily Dickinson." Incidental music by Rudolf Forst. Produced by Dave Schooler at the Vanderbilt Theatre, November 13, 1934. Staged by Clarence Derwent. Setting by P. Dodd Ackerman. With Earl McDonald, Helen Huberth, Helen Ray, Katherine Hirsch, Robert LeSueur, Edith Atwater, Herbert Warren, Albert van Dekker, Grant Gordon, Edward Ryan, Jr., Elizabeth Heaslip. Played Emily Dickinson.

1936

MAINLY FOR LOVERS. A comedy in three acts by Philip Johnson. Produced by Richard W. Krakeur and B. Charles Dean at the Forty-eighth Street Theatre, February 21, 1936. Staged by Harry Wagstaff Gribble. Setting by Clark Robinson. With Edgar Kent, Rachel Hartzell, Leo G. Carroll, Arthur Margetson. Played Helen Storer.

1936

RUSSET MANTLE a comedy in three acts by Lynn Riggs. Produced by Luther Greene. Directed by Alexander Dean. Dorothy toured in the summer theatres with Jay Fassett, Marshall Grant, Jeanne Casselle, Margaret Douglass, Charlotte McAleer, Robert Bentley, Ben Smith, Edmonia Nolley with smaller roles played by actors at each theatre. Played Kay Rowley.

1938

MISSOURI LEGEND. A comedy in three acts by E. B. Ginty. Produced by Guthrie McClintic in association with Max Gordon at the Empire Theatre, September 19, 1938. Staged by Guthrie McClintic. Settings by John Koenig. With Clare Woodbury, Jose Ferrer, Richard Bishop, Russell Collins, Karl Malden, Dan Duryea, Dean Jagger, Mildred Natwick, Joseph Sweeney, John Woodworth, Vincent Copeland, James Craig, John Philiber, Ben Roberts, Cliff Heckinger. Played Mrs. Howard.

1939

MORNING'S AT SEVEN. A comedy in three acts by Paul Osborn. Produced by Dwight Deere Wiman at the Longacre Theatre, November 30, 1939. Staged by Joshua Logan. Settings by Jo Mielziner. With Thomas Chalmers, Jean Adair, Kate McComb, Russell Collins, John Alexander, Enid Markey, Effie Shannon, Herbert Yost. Played Aaronetta Gibbs.

1940

LOVE FOR LOVE. A comedy in four acts by William Congreve. Prologue and epilogue by Charles Hanson Towne. Music by Macklin Marrow. Revived by The Players at the Hudson Theatre, June 3, 1940. Staged and designed by Robert Edmond Jones. Costumes by Millia Davenport. With Thomas H. Chalmers, Barry Jones, Leo G. Carroll, Edgar Stehli, Bobby Clark, Dudley Digges, Romney Brent, Herbert Ranson, A. G. Andrews, Paul Parks, Cornelia Otis Skinner, Peggy Wood, Violet Heming, Daisy Belmore, Jack Prescott, J. Ascher Smith, John Seymour, Neil Skinner, Richard Ellington, Jack Benwell. Singer: Evan Evans. Prologue: Walter Hampden. Epilogue: Cornelia Otis Skinner. Address during intermission: Otis Skinner. Played Miss Prue.

1940

LIFE WITH FATHER. A comedy in three acts by Howard Lindsay and Russel Crouse from the book by Clarence Day. Produced by Oscar Serlin. Staged by Bretaigne Windust. Settings and costumes by Stewart Chaney. (Dorothy toured for three years as well as replacing Dorothy Stickney in the New York company. As the boys outgrew their roles there were many replacements. At one point the cast consisted of the following players.) Viola Frayne, Peter Jamerson, Richard Noyes, Walter Kelly, Richard Hudson, Louis Calhern, Violet Holliday, Kay Lang, Toni Favor, Edwin Cushman, Mary Connelly, Hilda Woodrow, Marshall Bradford, James Jolley, Victoria Horne. Played Vinnie.

1942

THE GREAT BIG DOORSTEP. A comedy in three acts by Frances Goodrich and Albert Hackett from a novel by E. P. O'Connell. Produced by Herman Shumlin and staged by Mr. Shumlin at the Morosco Theatre, November 26, 1942. Setting by Howard Bay. With Joy Geffen, Jeanne Perkins Smith, Dickie Monahan, Gerald Matthews, Jack Manning, John Morny, Louis Calhern, Nat Burns, Ralph Bell, Clay Clement, Morton Stevens, Robert Crawley. Played Mrs. Crochet.

1944

OVER 21. Replaced the ailing star-author, Ruth Gordon, in Philadelphia as Paula Wharton as well as touring for the U.S.O. playing various military bases in this wartime comedy.

1946

THE MAGNIFICENT YANKEE. A comedy in three acts by Emmet Lavery. Produced by Arthur Hopkins at the Royale Theatre, January 22, 1946. Staged by Mr. Hopkins. Setting and costumes by Woodman Thompson. With Mason Curry, Louis Calhern, Fleming Ward, Christopher Marvin, Nicholas Saunders, Eleanor Swayne, William Roerick, Sherling Oliver, Philip Truex, Robert Healy, Edgar Barrier, Grey Stafford, Edward Hudson, Edwin Whitner, Bruce Bradford. Played Fanny Dixwell Holmes.

1947

THE STORY OF MARY SURRATT. A drama in three acts by John Patrick. Produced by Russell Lewis and Howard Young at Henry Miller's Theatre, February 8, 1947. Directed by John Patrick. Designed by Samuel Love. Lighting by Girvan Higginson. With Elizabeth Ross, Bernard Thomas, Don Shelton, Zachary Berger, Michael Fox, John Conway, James Monks, Grahan Denton, Larry Johns, Douglas McEachin, Richard Sanders, Wallis Roberts, Kent Smith, Edward Harvey, Frank McFarland, Robert Neff, Thomas Glynn, Robert Morgan, Dallas Boyd, Lee Malbourne, Arthur Stenning, Tom Daly, Gordon Barnes, Bill Hitch, John Pimley, Harlan Briggs, Hugh Mosher, Tom J. McGivern, Lytton Robinson, Bill Reynolds, Larry Johns, Earl Dawson, Michael Roane, Clyde Cook. Played Mary Surratt.

1950

THE MAN. A melodrama in two acts by Mel Dinelli. Produced by Kermit Bloomgarden at the Fulton Theatre, January 19, 1950. Staged by Martin Ritt. Setting and lighting by Jo Mielziner. Costumes by Julia Sze. With Don Hanmer, Peggy Ann Garner, Robert Emhardt, Frank McNellis, Josh White, Jr., Richard Boone. Played Mrs. Gillis.

1956

THE CHALK GARDEN. A play in three acts by Enid Bagnold. A Bowden, Barr and Bullock Production for a summer theatre tour. Staged by Charles Bowden, based on Sir John Gielgud's London production. Settings by Herman Rosse. With O. Z. Whitehead, Neil Fitzgerald, Frances Ingallis, Charron Follett. Two minor roles were played by actors from each local theatre. In one playhouse the young girl and her mother were played by Lee Remick and her mother. Lillian played Miss Madrigal and Dorothy played Mrs. St. Maugham.

Stageography

LILLIAN GISH

1930

UNCLE VANYA. A comedy in five acts by Anton Chekhov. Acting version by Rose Caylor. A Jed Harris production at the Booth Theatre, April 15, 1930, with supplementary engagement, September 22, 1930. Directed by Jed Harris. Settings by Jo Mielziner. With Kate Mayhew, Osgood Perkins, Walter Connolly, Zita Johann, Eugene Powers, Eduardo Ciannelli, Isabel Irving, Harold Johnsrud. Played Helena. (When the play reopened Zita Johann was replaced by Joanna Roos.)

1932

CAMILLE. A drama in three acts by Alexander Dumas. Produced by Delos Chappell for the re-opening of the Central City Opera House in Colorado in July of 1932 and opened at the Morosco Theatre in New York in November 1932. Production, direction, and settings by Robert Edmond Jones. Orchestra and special musical arrangement by Macklin Marrow. Miss Gish's costumes by Mr. Jones with Hilya Nordmark. With Cora Witherspoon, Helen Freeman, Mary Morris, Leona Boytel, Edna James, Raymond Hackett, Moffat Johnston, Frederick Worlock, Lewis Martin, Ian Wolfe, Ivan Bell, Arnold Ronnebeck, Paul Stephenson, Lili Montrachet, Eudora Vaughan, Marie Verneuil, Gabrielle Gelinas, Rene Crovenay, John Langrishe 3rd, Raoul Van Dyck, Lucien Porel, Jean Delanux, Raphael Ziem. Played Marguerite Gautier.

1933

NINE PINE STREET. A drama in six scenes and an epilogue by John Colton and Carlton Miles. Based on a play by William Miles and Donald Blackwell. Generously based on the Lizzie Borden murder case in Fall River, Massachusetts. Produced by Margaret Hewes. Staged by A. H. Van Buren. Settings and costumes by Robert Edmond Jones. With Helen Claire, Barna Ostertag, Janet Young, Eleanor Hicks, Robert Harrison, Raymond Hackett, Roberta Beatty, John H. Morrissey, Catherine Proctor, Jessamine Newcombe, William Ingersoll, James Hollicky, James P. Houston, Andree Corday, Clinton Sundberg. Played Effie Holden.

1934

THE JOYOUS SEASON. A comedy in three acts by Philip Barry. Produced by Arthur Hopkins at the Belasco Theatre, January 29, 1934. Staged by Mr. Hopkins. Setting by Robert Edmond Jones. With Eric Dressler, Jane Wyatt, Jerome Lawler, Barry Macollum, Alan Campbell, John Eldridge, Florence Williams, Moffat Johnston, Mary Kennedy, Kate Mayhew, Mary Hone. Played Christina Farley.

1934

WITHIN THE GATES. A symbolic drama in four scenes by Sean O'Casey. Produced by George Bushar and John Tuerk at the National Theatre, October 22, 1934. Staged by Melvyn Douglas. Setting by James Reynolds. Dance direction by Elsa Findlay. Incidental music by Milton Lusk and A. Lehman Engel. With Bramwell Fletcher, Moffat Johnston, Kathryn Collier, Barry Macollum, John Baly Murphy, Alexander Lewis, Morris Ankrum, Jessamine Newcombe, Ralph Sumpter, Miriam Goldina, Vera Fuller Mellish, Esther Mitchell, James Jolley, Barry Kelley, Edward Broadley, Arthur Villars, Baron McGrath, Ralph Cullinan, Mary Morris, Stanley G. Wood, Phil Bishop, Charles Angelo, Gordon Gould, Dodson Mitchell, Arthur Gould Porter, Charles Keane, Ellen Larned, Margaret Mower. Played the Young Whore.

1936

THE OLD MAID. A play in three acts by Zoe Akins from the novel by Edith Wharton. Presented by Charles B. Cochran in association with Howard and Wyndham Ltd., at the King's Theatre, Glasgow, March 2, 1936, and commenced to tour the provinces. Directed by Leontine Sagan. Designed by G. E. Calthrop. With Carol Goodner, Irene Vanbrugh, Harcourt Williams, Esma Cannon, Muriel Pavlow, Barbara Featherstone, Andrea Troubridge, Thelma Sheehan, Sheila Morris, Pamela Featherstone, Peggy Turner, Vera Hanson, Eric Mark, Maureen Glynne, Mona Harrison, Terence Neill, Sebastian Shaw, Carol Coombe, Patricia Burke, Kenneth Villiers, John Gatrell. Played Charlotte Lovell.

1936

HAMLET. A tragedy in two parts by William Shakespeare. Revived and staged by Guthrie McClintic at the Empire Theatre, October 8, 1936. Settings and costumes by Jo Mielziner. With Murvyn Vye, Reed Herring, Harry Andrews, Barry Kelly, Malcolm Keen, Whitner Bissell, James Dinan, John Emery, Arthur Byron, John Gielgud, Judith Anderson, John Cromwell, William Roehrick, Harry Mestayer, Ivan Triesault, Ruth March, George Vincent, William Stanley, George Nash, Morgan Farley, Evelyn Abbott, Neal Barry, John Galland, Stanley Gould, Peter Gray, Henry Hull, Jr., Mary Lee Logan, Donaldson Murphy, Sydna Scott, Kurt Steinbart. Played Ophelia.

1937

THE STAR WAGON. A dramatic fantasy in three acts by Maxwell Anderson. Produced and staged by Guthrie McClintic at the Empire Theatre, September 29, 1937. Settings by Jo Mielziner. With Russell Collins, Burgess Meredith, Whitner Bissell, Alan Anderson, Muriel Starr, Howard Freeman, Kent Smith, Barry Kelley, Charles Forrester, John Philiber, Jane Buchanan, J. Arthur Young, Mildred Natwick, Edmund O'Brien, Evelyn Abbott, Edith Smither, William Garner. Played Martha Minch.

1939

DEAR OCTOPUS. A comedy in three acts by Dodie Smith. Produced by John C. Wilson at the Broadhurst Theatre, January 11, 1939. Staged by Glen Byam Shaw. Settings by G. E. Calthrop. With Reginald Mason, Lucile Watson, Phyllis Joyce, Phyllis Povah, Rose Hobart, Jack Hawkins, Peter Robinson, Shirley Poirier, Warren Mills, Helen Renee, Ivy Troutman, Robert Craven, Naomi Campbell, Margaret Dale, Alice Belmore Cliffe, Georgia Harvey. Played Grace (Fenny) Fenning.

1939

LIFE WITH FATHER. A comedy in three acts by Howard Lindsay and Russel Crouse from the book by Clarence Day. Produced by Oscar Serlin. Staged by Bretaigne Windust. Setting and costumes by Stewart Chaney. After a preliminary tour in 1939, it opened at the Blackstone Theatre, Chicago, February 19, 1940. It ran a record sixty-six weeks, closing May 24, 1941. With Percy Waram, O. Z. Whitehead, Virgilia Chew, Georgette McKee, George LeSoir, Peter Jamerson, Jimmy Roland, David Jeffries, Clara Joel, Margaret Randall, Carroll Ashburn, Camelia Campbell, Edwin Cushman, Aubrey Hynes, Gertrude Beach. Played Vinnie.

1942

MR. SYCAMORE. A comedy in eight scenes by Ketti Frings based on a story by Robert Ayre. Produced by the Theatre Guild at the Guild Theatre, November 13, 1942. Staged by Lester Vail. Supervised by Theresa Helburn and Lawrence Langner. Settings by Samuel Leve. With Harry Townes, Harry Sheppard, Stuart Erwin, Leona Powers, John Philiber, Enid Markey, Louise McBride, Buddy Swan, Walter Appler, Franklyn Fox, Russell Collins, Otto Hulett, Ernest Theiss, Kenneth Hayden, Rupert Pole, Albert Bergh, Mary Heckart, Jed Dooley, Pearl Herzog, Ray J. Largay, Harry Vellaver. Played Jane Gwilt.

1947

THE MARQUISE. A play by Noel Coward. Toured the summer theatres as a package show carrying the following actors: John Williams, Judson Laire, Mary MacArthur, Robert Vetault and again toured in 1948 with the following actors: John Williams, Judson Laire, Sonny Adams, William Hunt. At each theatre the company would add the additional actors from the resident members.

1947

CRIME AND PUNISHMENT. A drama in two acts by Feodor Dostoyevsky. Dramatized by Rodney Ackland. Produced by Robert Whitehead and Oliver Rea at the National Theatre, December 22, 1947. Directed by Theodore Komisarjevsky. Associate Producer, Bea Lawrence. Settings by Paul Sherriff. Costumes by Lester Polakov. With Ben Morse, Dolly Haas, Betty Lou Keim, Sherry Smith, Paton Price, Elisabeth Neumann, Howard Fischer, Wauna Paul, Robert Donley, Scott Moore, Michael Arshansky, Galina Talva, Susan Steell, Mary James, John Gielgud, Sanford Meisner, Alexander Scourby, Richard Purdy, E. A. Krumschmidt, Alice John, Marian Seldes, Vladimir Sokoloff, Mort Marshall, Patrick McVey, William Beal, David Elliott, Cecile Sherman, Amy Douglass, Jeri Souvinet, Eugenia Woods, Arthur Griffin, Richard Hayes, Mary Diveny, Mary Stuart, Marjorie Tas, Neils Miller, Robert Pastene, Graham Ferguson, John Vicari, Theodore Tenley, James Matsagas, Sandy Campbell. Played Katrina Ivanna.

1948

THE LEGEND OF LEONORA. A play in three acts by J. M. Barrie. Presented by Mrs. Walter Hartwig at the Ogunquit Playhouse the week of August, 16, 1948, in Ogunquit, Maine. Directed by Wesley McKee. Setting by Robert MacKichan. With Joan Bower, William Swetland, Caroline Marshall, Ronald Graham, G. Swayne Gordon, Noel Leslie, Randolph Sauerherring, Carl Benton Reid, John Davis, John Shugrue, Emil Kovach, Stephen Prouty, Daisy Atherton, Jerry Stout, Wallis Howe. Played Leonora.

1948

MRS. CARLYLE. A historical play in three acts by Glenn Hughes. Presented at the Showboat Theatre, University of Washington, Seattle, October 7, 1948, under the personal supervision of the author. Directed by Kenneth Carr. Settings by John Ashby Conway. Costumes by Lucy Barton. (The play ran fifty-one performances, a record for noncommercial theatre.) With Ruth Balkema Prins, Chris Hansen, Ogaenia Calkings, Dolores Heath, Wayne Carson, Jeff Forsythe, Robert Gray, Robert Cass, Jack Wright, Marion Hayes Cass, Stuart Currie, Thomas Dargan, Gloria Wingert, Nann Ballard, Robert Prins, Mary Jasperson. Played Jane Welsh.

1950

MISS MABEL. A play in three acts by R. C. Sherriff. Produced by Joel Schenker as a summer theatre touring package. Advance director: Jerome Coray. With Charles Francis, Wallace Clark, Mark Roberts, Harry Bannister, Victor Beecroft, Gwen Anderson, Marie Carroll, Bethell Long. Subsequent cast changes throughout tour as well as resident actors playing different roles at each theatre.

1950

THE CURIOUS SAVAGE. A comedy in three acts by John Patrick. Produced by The Theatre Guild and Lewis and Young at the Martin Beck Theatre, October 24, 1950. Directed by Peter Glenville. Designed and lighted by George Jenkins. Costumes by Anna Hill Johnstone. With Isobel Elsom, Robert Emhardt, Lois Hall, Hugh Reilly, Gladys Henson, Brandon Peters, Howard Wendell, Marta Linden, Flora Campbell, Sydney Smith. Played Ethel.

1953

THE TRIP TO BOUNTIFUL. A play in three acts by Horton Foote. Produced by The Theatre Guild and Fred Coe at Henry Miller's Theatre, November 3, 1953. Directed by Vincent J. Donehue. Settings by Otis Riggs. Costumes by Rose Bogdanoff. Lighting by Peggy Clark. With Gene Lyons, Jo Van Fleet, Eva Marie Saint, Will Hare, Salem Ludwig, David Clive, Frederic Downs, Frank Overton, Patricia MacDonald, Neil Laurence, Helen Cordes. Played Mrs. Carrie Watts.

1956

THE CHALK GARDEN. (See the Stageography of Dorothy Gish.)

1957

Opening of Congress Hall in West Berlin, Germany, September 19, 1957, under the auspices of the Benjamin Franklin Foundation. Opening speakers included Lord Mayor Otto Suhr of Berlin, Mrs. Clare Boothe Luce, Robert Dowling, David K. E. Bruce, U.S. Ambassador to Germany. Soprano Eileen Farrell made her European concert debut. Martha Graham danced William Schuman's "Judith" with Virgil Thomson conducting the RIAS Orchestra of Berlin. On September 20, under the sponsorship of ANTA, Thornton Wilder spoke and the following actors performed in seven one-act plays: Lillian Gish, Eileen Heckart, Ethel Waters, Burgess Meredith, Hiram Sherman, Bill Gunn, Billie Allen, Richard Ward, John Becher, James Daly, Cynthia Baxter, Vinie Burrows. Gertrude Macy staged the inaugural week's events. Lillian Gish starred in Tennessee Williams' "Portrait of a Madonna" and was directed by Lamont Johnson in Thornton Wilder's "The Wreck on the 5:25" with Burgess Meredith and Mr. Wilder.

1958

THE FAMILY REUNION. The first American professional production of the verse play in two acts by T. S. Eliot at the Phoenix Theatre, October 20, 1958. Managing Directors T. Edward Hambleton and Norris Houghton. Directed by Stuart Vaughan. Setting by Norris Houghton. Costumes and lighting by Will Steven Armstrong. Music composed by David Amram. With Florence Reed, Dorothy Sands, Margaretta Warwick, Nicholas Joy, Eric Berry, Sylvia Short, Fritz Weaver, Christine Thomas, Robert Geiringer, Conrad Bain, Meredith Dallas. Played Agatha.

1960

ALL THE WAY HOME. A drama in three acts by Tad Mosel. Based on the novel A Death in the Family by James Agee. Produced by Fred Coe in association with Arthur Cantor at the Belasco Theatre, November 30, 1960. Directed by Arthur Penn. Settings and lighting by David Hays. Costumes by Raymond Sovey. With John Megna, Larry Provost, Jeff Conaway, Gary Morgan, Robert Ader, Arthur Hill, Colleen Dewhurst, Clifton James, Lenka Peterson, Edwin Wolfe, Georgia Simmons, Christopher Month, Dorrit Kelton, Lylah Tiffany, Aline MacMahon, Thomas Chalmers, Tom Wheatley, Art Smith. Played Catherine Lynch.

1963

A PASSAGE TO INDIA. A drama in two acts by Santha Rama Rau from the novel by E. M. Forster. Presented at the Goodman Theatre, Chicago, Illinois, January 11, 1963. Directed by Charles McGaw. Settings by James Maronek. Costumes by Caley Summers. Lighting by G. E. Naselius. With David Britton, Michael Thompson, Saadoun Al-Bayati, Jerry Hillmer, Wilma Ostergaard, Ibrahim Jalal, Edward Moore, Robert Jacobson, Charles Geraci, Carolyn Dry, Lane Corvey, Sondra Hirsch, Larry Adams, James Chudnow, Roy Clary, Herb Felsenfeld, Dan Clifford, Leo Maroules, Anthony Corso, Badry Fareed, Lynda Bobbitt, Judy Friedenberg, Jan Ricciarelli, Leonore Terrutty, Jody Lester. Played Mrs. Moore.

1963

TOO TRUE TO BE GOOD. A modern comedy by George Bernard Shaw. Revived by Paul Vroom, Buff Cobb, and Burry Fredrik at the 54th Street Theatre, March 12, 1963. Directed by Albert Marre. Settings and lighting by Paul Morrison. Costumes by Edith Lutyens Bel Geddes. Incidental music by Mitch Leigh. Transition sequences designed by Abner Dean. Associate Producer Robert M. Newsom. With Sir Cedric Hardwicke, Eileen Heckart, Glynis Johns, Ray Middleton, Robert Preston, Cyril Ritchard, David Wayne. Played Mrs. Mopply.

1965

ROMEO AND JULIET. A tragedy in five acts by William Shakespeare. Presented by the American Shakespeare Festival, Stratford, Connecticut, June 20, 1965. Produced by Joseph Verner Reed. Artistic Director Allen Fletcher. Associate Producer Berenice Weiler. Directed by Allen Fletcher. Scenery by Will Steven Armstrong. Lighting by Tharon Musser. Costumes by Ann Roth. Songs and music by Conrad Susa. Musical Director Jose Serebrier. Choreography by William Burdick. Duels staged by Christopher Tanner. With Robert Benedict, Nick Smith, Richard Kuss, Edwin Owens, Richard Morse, Theodore Sorel, Dennis Jones, Ted Graeber, Richard Mathews, Josef Sommer, Patricia Hamilton, John Carpenter, Mary Hara, Todd Drexel, Terence Scammell, Deveren Bookwalter, David Grimm, Maria Tucci, Geneva Bugbee, John Cunningham, Patrick Hines, Thomas Ruisinger. Played the Nurse to Juliet.

1965

ANYA. A musical in two acts. Produced by Fred R. Fehlhaber at the Ziegfeld Theatre, November 29, 1965. Book by George Abbott and Guy Bolton. Based upon "Anastasia" by Marcelle Maurette and Guy Bolton. Music and lyrics by Robert Wright and George Forrest. Based on themes by S. Rachmaninoff. Directed by George Abbott. Choreography and musical numbers by Hanya Holm. Scenery by Robert Randolph. Costumes by Patricia Zipprodt. Lighting by Richard Casler. Musical Direction by Harold Hastings. Orchestrations by Don Walker. With Constance Towers, Patricia Hoffman, Michael Kermoyan, Boris Aplon, Lawrence Brooks, Adair McGowan, Jack Dabdoub, Walter Hook, Irra Petina, Ed Steffe, Konstantin Pio-Ulsky, Karen Shepard, George S. Irving, Laurie Franks, Rita Metzger, Lawrence Boyll, Elizabeth Howell, Barbara Alexander, Maggie Task, Michael Quinn, John Michael King, Bernard Frank, Howard Kahl, Margaret Mullen, Ciya Challis, Patricia Drylie, Juliette Durand, Kip Andrews, Steven Boockvor, Randy Doney, Joseph Nelson, Mia Powers, Lourette Raymon, Diane Tarleton, Darrel Askey, Les Freed, Horace Guittard, Richard Nieves, J. Vernon Oaks, Robert Sharp, John Taliaferro. Played the Dowager Empress.

1968

I NEVER SANG FOR MY FATHER. A drama in two acts by Robert Anderson. Produced by Gilbert Cates in Association with Doris Vidor at the Longacre Theatre, January 25, 1968. Directed by Alan Schneider. Scenery and lighting by Jo Mielziner. Costumes by Theoni V. Aldredge. With Hal Holbrook, Earl Sydnor, Alan Webb, Sloane Shelton, Laurinda Barrett, Allan Frank, Matt Crowley, James A. Spearman, Daniel Keyes, Teresa Wright. Played Margaret Garrison.

1973

UNCLE VANYA. Scenes from Country Life in Four Acts by Anton Chekhov. Translated by Albert Todd and Mike Nichols. Presented by Circle in the Square, Inc., Theodore Mann, Artistic Director, Paul Libin, Managing Director, at the Circle in the Square-Joseph E. Levine Theatre. Previews began May 21, 1973. Opened June 4, 1973, for a limited engagement. Directed by Mike Nichols. Designed by Tony Walton. Lighting by Jules Fisher. With George C. Scott, Julie Christie, Nicol Williamson, Elizabeth Wilson, Cathleen Nesbitt, Barnard Hughes, Conrad Bain, Rod Loomis, Tom Tarpey, R. Mack Miller. Played Marina, the nurse.

To be continued